"Brock Morgan has the rare combination of empathy, wisdom, and extensive experience in youth ministry, making him a trusted voice in the conversation about a struggle too many teenagers face: anxiety. Brock speaks with both expertise and vulnerability as he shares about his own battle with anxiety and reminds us that if we are a good steward of our pain, even our deepest heartache can be an avenue of Christ's transformation in our lives and offer hope to others. As a marriage and family therapist who has worked with countless teenagers suffering from anxiety, I am thankful for Brock's wise voice and will be keeping a stack of copies of this book in my office as a valuable resource for families touched by this particular brand of pain. Join me in underlining the whole thing."
—Nicole Zasowski, Licensed Marriage and Family Therapist and Author of *What If It's Wonderful?*

"Anxiety among teens is escalating at a daunting rate. What's going on? Everyone who cares about kids is concerned about the staggering rise in teen depression and anxiety. Brock Morgan has worked with teens for over 30 years. He is a student of their culture, and he understands. I love how he uses his own life experiences to help us get into the mind and heart of today's adolescents. This is a great and insightful read."
—Jim Burns, Ph.D., President of HomeWord and Author of *Understanding Your Teen* and *Doing Life with Your Adult Children: Keep Your Mouth Shut and the Welcome Mat Out*

"If there was ever a time that we needed a book like this, it is now. Adolescents are facing incredible anxiety issues. Our adult culture adds high anxiety to the youth culture. Seems like everyone is stressed out. The number one prescribed drug for teens and young adults today is anti-anxiety medication. Brock Morgan has done a great job in moving us miles ahead of simple clichés and solutions.

I don't normally use alliteration, but as I took notes on his book, three words came to my mind: personal, profound, and practical. If you work with teenagers, whether you're a youth worker, parent, mental health counselor, schoolteacher, coach, or anyone else who is invested in this generation of students, Brock Morgan's book is for you! This will be a great asset in helping you with anxious teenagers."
—Dr. David Olshine, Professor and Director of Youth Ministry, Family, and Culture at Columbia International University

"I have sat across the table from Brock and he lives out what he writes. This book is absolutely brilliant and so necessary because it covers so many of the obstacles young people face, from the daily fears to cyberbullying to panic attacks... I believe this is a must-read for anyone who cares about this next generation and I'm very grateful that Brock took the time to write it for us."
—Dan Blythe, Global Youth Director, Alpha International

"Teenagers are walking around in survival mode and youth ministry leaders have an opportunity to walk with them to safety and wholeness. But how? Brock gives incredibly practical and solid insight from his own experiences to anyone who wants to help today's teenagers flourish and make it through to the other side. Brock is an expert in youth culture and he gives leaders great help to intentionally learn about the ways anxiety impacts and harms teenagers in our communities. Then, he offers ideas for how to collectively respond to the needs that we see. This book is a MUST read for anyone who cares about this next generation."
—Brooklyn Lindsey, Author, Speaker, and Pastor at SOMOS Church

"Brock Morgan is one of those rare youth workers who has had a tremendous long game in youth ministry. I trust him and I'm excited for this book to get into the hands of all youth workers. He tackles critical issues that we must address and he does it with his personal credibility and his passion to help those of us who care for teenagers. I'm so grateful for his help and recommend this to anyone who cares about the next generation."
—Doug Fields, Pastor, Author, and Cofounder of DownloadYouthMinistry.com

"Those of us who work with young people see all too clearly what is happening with anxiety. It can be jarring to read the statistics and even scarier as a parent to see it in your home or as a leader in your youth group. Fortunately, Brock has addressed this overwhelming topic with an amazing amount of hope. He comes to us with his experiences and offers us a way forward. If you care about and want to understand what is happening in the hearts and minds of our youth this is a great place to start."
—Josh Griffin, Junior High Pastor and Cofounder of DownloadYouthMinistry.com

"As someone who struggles with anxiety and has sought counseling, AND as someone who has worked with students for the last fifteen years, this book, the research, and the applications from Brock are just so vital. This will be an incredible resource to anyone working with Gen Z and Gen Alpha."
—Justin Knowles, Family Pastor at Sandals Church, Riverside, CA

"Brock Morgan's book *The Anxious Teen* is insightful, challenging, and full of hope. A must-read for any youth worker, or person who longs to see young people know the transformative power of Jesus."
—Tom Clark, Youth Director and Holy Trinity Brompton Live Stream Pastor

"As a former youth pastor of twenty years and now a full-time licensed mental health counselor, I wish I would have had this as a resource from the start. This book should be mandatory reading for people working with teens and parents. Brock and Hallie provide us with great advice and chapter after chapter of practical ways to help students who wrestle with anxiety. Just as important are their words of wisdom on how youth ministers can engage their own anxiety and lean toward a youth ministry that highlights vulnerability and empathy."
—Nate Rice, MA, LHMC

"You might argue with Brock Morgan's take on the history of adolescence in America, but don't for a moment doubt his compassion for teenagers and parents, his courage in disclosing his own vulnerabilities, or his practical advice on helping kids with anxiety. The last word in every chapter, from family therapist Hallie Scott, annotates how attentive youth workers can learn to help teenagers find what they need to live through and maybe even beyond anxiety."
—Jim Hancock, Author and Content Designer

"This is the best book I have ever read."
—Carol Morgan (Brock's Mom)

THE ANXIOUS TEEN

Ministry With Stressed and Fearful Students

BROCK MORGAN
with HALLIE SCOTT, MFT

The Anxious Teen

Copyright © 2022 by Brock Morgan
Publisher: Mark Oestreicher
Managing Editor: Sarah Hauge
Cover Design and Layout: Marilee Pankratz
Creative Director: Moaning Myrtle

ISBN-13: 978-1-942145-68-4

The Youth Cartel, LLC
www.theyouthcartel.com
Email: info@theyouthcartel.com
Born in San Diego.
Printed worldwide.

CONTENTS

SOUNDTRACK

I always like to include in my books a list of the music that inspired
and encouraged the writing. I have a hard time even getting a
word out without music playing.

So here is this book's soundtrack that kept me company.

Joshua Luke Smith - *The Void*

Larkin Poe - *Paint the Roses* & *Kindred Spirits*

Thrice - *Horizons/East*

Inhaler - *My Honest Face*

Jon Foreman - *Departures*

Foo Fighters - *Medicine at Midnight*

OneRepublic - *Human*

Wilder Woods

311 - *Essentials*

BROODS - *Space Island*

NEEDTOBREATHE - *Into the Mystery*

Coldplay - *Music of the Spheres*

Taylor Swift - *Folklore*

Switchfoot - *Interrobang*

Pearl Jam - *Gigaton*

Flag Day (Original Soundtrack)

Eddie Vedder - *Earthling*

DEDICATION

To teenagers everywhere who are struggling.

AUTHOR'S NOTE

If you've recently turned on the TV or read anything about teenagers today, you might think, "Man, it's over! These kids don't have a chance. They're a mess!"

But if you've ever sat across the table from a teenager and really listened to them, I bet you were surprised by their depth, their heart, and the way they see themselves and the world. If you knew teens like I do, I think you'd discover that our greatest hope lies within the potential of these hurting, sensitive, and anxious young people.

I have spoken at youth conferences, camps, and retreats for decades, but I've never had to work so little at convincing teenagers that the way of the world is leading us to dysfunction and brokenness. Today's teens already know this. They may not know that the way of Jesus leads them to life, but they certainly know that this culture is leading us away from wholeness. More on this later.

The following pages are a joint effort intended to bring clarity, information, practical insight, and hope as you work with anxious teenagers. I hope you'll be encouraged, surprised, and challenged all along the way.

When I first began to tackle this project two years ago, it felt overwhelming and dark and dismal. I wasn't really sure I wanted to take a deep dive into the topic of teens and anxiety. But as a youth worker in today's world, I'm already in it. I couldn't give up. And truthfully, the longer I worked and the more time I spent with Generation Z and Generation Alpha, the more hope-filled I became. Because of the complexity and nuance of this topic, I enlisted the help of brilliant marriage and family therapist Hallie Scott, someone who has unique qualifications for making sure I'm not putting more stupid out into the world. She is also uniquely qualified to help us understand what is really going on in the lives of young people. She brings her years of experience as a counselor to offer incredible insight on this topic. Hallie will end each chapter with a thoughtful response from her perspective as a therapist. I am super grateful for her friendship and partnership. I imagine that I'm not the easiest person to work with. As an

THE ANXIOUS TEEN

Enneagram 7, just getting me to write cohesive chapters is quite a chore (thank you Sarah Hauge for your amazing editing job).

My hope is that this will be one of the most practical and hopeful reads you will encounter about the unique challenges of young people and mental health today. As a youth worker, joining God in lifting kids' heads away from shame for the past thirty-plus years has been my amazing privilege. I absolutely love what I do. So go ahead and turn the page. Let's do this!

The Gift of Anxiety

I began my youth ministry career in 1991 as a youth intern. It's hard to believe that I've been in youth work now for over thirty years. Some moments have been full of wonder and exhilaration while others have been characterized by dashed hopes and a broken heart. Most of my thirty-plus years of ministry have taken place inside the walls of the church. Not only have I given my adult life to it, but the church is also where I, as a pastor's kid, spent much of my childhood. It's been a lot, and it's no wonder that I have a bit of PTSD. But I'm grateful for it all. I'm even grateful for the personal anxiety that has erupted in my life as a result of my experiences. I remember clearly when that anxiety first reared its ugly head.

"Brock, are you okay? Sweetie, what's going on?" my wife, Kelsey, asked as she knocked on our locked bedroom door.

Truth is, I didn't know what was going on. All I knew is that I was having a hard time breathing.

I was working at what I thought was my dream job at a massive megachurch with great influence. When they offered me the gig, I was instantly excited to say yes—but my always insightful wife had serious hesitations.

"I'm just not sure about the pastor. He didn't even speak to us at the luncheon when we were interviewing. Plus, I didn't like how they called the people who attend the church 'customers.'"

THE ANXIOUS TEEN

I shrugged. "Well, he must have liked us. They offered me the job. But the customer thing, well, yeah okay, that actually was weird."

Despite her concerns, I did my best to convince Kelsey that everything was going to be just fine. After all, this is what we'd been working for all of these years.

Ignorance is bliss—until it isn't.

My first day on the job was a Sunday. I stood at the entrance of the youth building welcoming in students. I was so excited to meet them, and they seemed thrilled to meet the new youth pastor. I was pumped!

And then a man walked up behind me and tapped my shoulder.

"Hey, um, are you the youth pastor here?"

"I am," I said with a smile.

"Well, I wanted to give you a heads up about something. I was in a meeting yesterday that kept me awake all night afterward. I just felt impressed to come and speak to you about it."

"Okay man, what's going on?" I questioned.

"Well," he said, "I was in a meeting with a few of the pastors and elders yesterday and the lead pastor mentioned that he was really unhappy with the direction that you're taking the youth group."

I quickly interrupted. "Dude, this is my first day working here. I haven't even unpacked my office yet."

"Is your name Brock Morgan?" he asked.

"Yeah..."

"Well, that's who he was talking about. I felt like I was supposed to give you a warning. And please know that I'll be praying for you."

He shook my hand and I never saw him again. To this day I don't know if he was an elder at the church or what. I dismissed this interaction, deciding he must have been confused. There's no way what he said could be true. That guy must have mixed up my name with someone else's or something.

But over the next few weeks I kept hearing from people that the lead pastor was saying negative things about me behind closed doors. Each time this happened, the lump that had formed in my throat grew larger. I didn't know what to do, so I mentioned what was going on to my dear friend over at Youth Specialties, Tic Long.

"You need to confront him and get everything out on the table," Tic said. This was good advice. So I scheduled a face-to-face meeting with the lead pastor through his admin—only to have our meeting cancelled the day of. I rescheduled—and it got cancelled again. And this kept happening for the next six months.

I went to another pastor on staff and told him what was going on. I'll never forget what happened next.

He put his hands on my shoulders and looked me square in the face.

"Brock," he said, "you're in a no-win situation. You are not the lead pastor's pick. Everyone wanted to hire you except for him. I think he might be trying to sabotage you."

Say what?!

I felt sick. *This is insane!* I thought.

"If I were you I'd ask the executive pastor to get a meeting together and just talk it through," the other pastor advised. So that's exactly what I did.

Two weeks later I found myself sitting at a coffee shop with the executive pastor, two associate pastors, and the lead pastor. I felt like I was looking across the table at the heads of the mafia, or like Tom Cruise in the movie *The Firm*. It was strange, nerve-wracking, and scary. I was hoping they couldn't see my heart pounding inside my chest as I looked directly at the lead pastor and laid it out there.

"Look, I've only been here six months and we can call it quits if I'm not your guy. Just say the word. I can get another job. You don't need me here if you'd rather have someone else."

I'm not sure what I expected, but it wasn't what he said next. "Oh no, Brock, you're our guy. I want you to succeed."

"Well then, why am I hearing from people that you don't think I'm a good fit? That you're unhappy with the direction of the youth ministry? Look man, just be honest. I can take it," I said.

"No, I mean it, Brock. You're my guy and I want you to do well here."

After that meeting I hoped for the best…but more of the same continued. I began to feel the lump move from my throat to my chest. It was an unsafe feeling. I felt it every time I drove onto the church property. In every meeting and every conversation it was there, always present. The feeling became a constant ache deep inside of me, a pit in my stomach, a deep hurt and a tightening in my chest.

At the time, I didn't really know what anxiety was. People didn't talk about it much during those days. But anxiety is exactly what I was experiencing.

Back to me in the locked bedroom:

"Brock, are you okay? Sweetie, what's going on?"

I wasn't doing okay.

In fact, I was barely hanging on. Work was incredibly stressful and it was impacting me, all the time. Every youth group the executive pastor would walk in during my talk and stand in the back of the auditorium counting heads. I'd continue with my talk as best I could, but I was dying inside.

I learned that the place was a pressure cooker, even separate from the pastor speaking negatively about me. Everyone felt it at least a little bit. Numbers, numbers, numbers was all they spoke about. How to keep the "customers" happy and make sure they kept coming back was a prominent theme in staff meetings. All of it began to wear me down. Still, I did my best and the youth group was growing. When we took a group of students and leaders to Mexico for a mission trip, it was the largest group they had ever taken. Even this wasn't enough to assuage the concerns or lessen the negativity.

I spent only a couple of years at the church before it was too much. I reluctantly signed an agreement saying that I would never mention the church's name, and in return they'd pay me four months' severance to walk away. And walk away I did, but I was a mess.

A few months later my incredible wife made me go to a counselor. One afternoon she looked at me and said, "Brock, you're not the man I married. You're bitter and angry, and you're mean."

The thing is, she was right.

I needed help. That tightening in my chest was now there all of the time, to one degree or another. Shortening my breath. Always present, always pressing in.

A couple of weeks later I was sitting in my counselor's office when she asked a question.

"Who do you need to forgive, even if they're not asking you for forgiveness?"

I just looked at her. "Nope," I said after a moment. "I want that guy to pay." Forgiveness? No thanks. I left our session with great resolve to not only *not* forgive the lead pastor, but to spread the word as much as I could about all of the youth workers and ministers whom he had deeply injured over his many years in ministry. And the list, I had come to learn, was huge!

THE ANXIOUS TEEN

What I didn't realize was that by holding on to this bitterness, I was only hurting myself.

Two years later I found myself sitting in a chapel service in a different town listening to my father—who, remember, is a pastor—talk about forgiveness.

Forgiveness. At that point, this was a word I'd avoided for almost three years. I was exhausted and at the end of my rope. I was miserable. Time had passed, but I was still carrying anxiety and bitterness. I sat there listening to my dad speak when, finally, something happened. Oftentimes a breakdown needs to happen before a breakthrough, and that's what I experienced that morning. I broke down.

"God, help me to forgive. I don't know how to do it. I don't know how to let go. But I know that you do. Please help me."

It didn't happen instantly, but over the next couple of years I felt that burden of unforgiveness slowly lift off of me. That was huge. What I didn't realize at the time, though, was that this didn't change my relationship with anxiety. The damage had been done and anxiety had become a permanent part of my life.

Kelsey and I took a job across the country. We were excited to move to a bedroom community just outside of New York City. The church had promised me that I could hire two people to work on the youth ministry staff with me, and had agreed that I could start an internship program. On my first day of work I was full of vigor and excitement. I told the executive pastor that I had spoken with a couple of staff candidates I was excited about.

"Oh, you didn't hear?" he answered nonchalantly. "We took those positions out of the budget. Maybe down the road if you build this ministry and a bunch of kids start coming, then maybe you might be able to hire someone part-time. Maybe."

I was flabbergasted. I didn't know what to do.

It felt like a bait and switch. Actually, it *was* a bait and switch.

This felt wrong. But I had just moved my family across the country. So I put my head and down worked my tail off. For the next nine months, I worked late into the evenings and through the weekends. I didn't take time off. I was running the middle school group separate from the high school group, and I started a student leadership program. And then on top of all of that, the church asked me to launch a young adult service on Sunday evenings. I said yes.

The youth group was growing and God was working and Sunday nights were amazing and from the outside, everything looked great. But inside I was hurting, struggling, and barely staying afloat. I was on the verge of falling apart. I was doing everything I could not to fall apart.

One evening I was getting ready for a prayer meeting at the church, preparing for my part in the service. All of a sudden I started hyperventilating and sweating. My heart was pounding out of control. I knew that I was dying. This was it, I was having a heart attack. Kelsey and our daughter, Dancin, were there with me, and I gasped, weeping, struggling to tell them how much I loved them. I really thought I was speaking my final words. I remember the fear in their eyes as I said my last goodbyes, tears running down our faces.

Dude! It was quite a scene.

When we got to the hospital I found out it wasn't a heart attack at all. I'd actually had a panic attack. I was both relieved and terrified.

Am I crazy?

- I didn't know how to fix this.
- I didn't know how to be well.
- I didn't know how to do anything.

And I didn't feel safe to tell my boss or anyone else at the church what was going on.

THE ANXIOUS TEEN

So I just kept going.

The couple of years around this time were difficult. When I hear my daughter talk about them now, it makes me really emotional. I hate that she remembers me in that state. I hate that she remembers my temper and my out of control, erratic behavior. It wasn't until my wife pushed me a second time to get into counseling that healing and wholeness began to come my way.

By that point I had reached the end of my rope, so I was wide open to counseling, desperate for anything that might help me. I began meeting with a counseling student from the seminary down the road because he was free (a plus for any youth worker) and he needed the hours to get his degree. It was mutually beneficial and we took full advantage. And from the first moment we met, I felt hope.

The counseling LITERALLY saved me.
- It saved my marriage.
- It saved my faith.
- It saved my relationship with my daughter.
- It saved my ministry.
- It saved me.

And after a few months of getting the help I needed, the anxiety that had once felt like a curse began to feel like a gift. This became clear when more and more students in our youth group began to struggle with deep anxiety. The gift was that I could relate to them. I could empathize with them. They were, on the regular, experiencing the same symptoms I had. Many students from our group were experiencing heart attack-like palpitations, balling up on the floor in their locked bedrooms, unable to function. I had been there.

I became a student of my own condition. I knew I could help them. As God redeemed my own circumstances, I began to see my own anxiety as my secret superpower. Isn't it funny that it can work that way? I don't believe that God brought anxiety into my life—my theology doesn't tell me that. But my theology *does* tell me that God so loved me and the world that he would do anything, go to great lengths, to rescue me. As I have learned, human anxiety was actually built in by a loving Creator to warn us when our minds and bodies are experiencing negative, difficult, or unsafe circumstances. Anxiety was designed to keep us safe. Anxiety in itself is not necessarily bad. In fact, back in thosedays my anxiety was a last-ditch effort by my brain and my body to get me to change something, to rest, and to seek health. My anxiety helped me to see that I needed help. Counseling helped me to see that anxiety, like all things, is redeemable. God has used it in my life and in the lives of those I have the privilege of ministering to. I'm profoundly grateful.

Writing this now is strange for me, but it is true: Experiencing anxiety has become one of my greatest gifts.

My journey with anxiety has continued. I've never been cured and I've never had an easy church experience. Never. Churches are tough places to work. But they are also vehicles God has chosen to help bring hope, healing, wholeness, grace, and love into the world. And the cool thing is that the world has never been more desperate for all of that than it is right now.

CHAPTER TAKEAWAYS

- Anxiety is tenacious. We can try to ignore it, but it won't go away.
- Any of us can begin to experience life-affecting anxiety at any age or stage.
- Despite the many challenges it brings, anxiety can also be a superpower.

NOTES *from a Mental Health Therapist*

What strikes me in Brock's story is his ability to see his anxiety as a superpower. I think he is the first person I've met who sees it that way, and I think it's great. Brock was able to recognize the anxiety for what it is: an incongruence. His anxiety meant that something wasn't adding up. For Brock this was a work situation that didn't make sense, and he was trying really hard to make it make sense.

Brock did what so many of us do: We feel excited and even relieved when we have the opportunity to say yes to that "perfect" thing we have been working so hard for—and then we are hit with the reality that it isn't actually perfect. This creates a conflict, the incongruence I mentioned before. We wonder what's causing the conflict. Is it because this thing is not as great as I thought? Am I not fit for the task? And if I am not fit for this task, what does *that* mean? Have I been lying to myself about my abilities? Self-doubt rears its ugly head. And then what?

Brock fought hard to make his amazing job the thing that he had built up in his mind, but the reality is that it just wasn't. This incongruence, which caused an internal fight full of conflicting thoughts, created Brock's anxiety. I love in this story that Kelsey was able to speak into Brock's fight, and I love that Brock was able to hear it.

Sometimes we don't have such a straightforward answer for what is causing our anxiety. Sometimes we feel the anxiety come out of nowhere. This can create a toxic loop of increasing concern. As we try to figure out what is causing our anxiety and are unable to do so, it creates even more anxiety.

Many of us hold tight to the belief that if we can figure out what is causing our anxiety, then the anxiety will go away. This is usually a lie. We often need to allow the anxiety to be felt before it can dissipate, which is uncomfortable. Or, we need to take steps to get help, like Brock did.

What I love most about what Brock shared is that he allowed Dancin to witness the process of a parent seeking help when needed. So many parents worry that showing their child anything that might be considered a negative emotion will cause damage. As a result, parents often try to hide these feelings. They work to pretend that everything is okay. But ironically, hiding things is what causes fear. Teaching our kids, even indirectly, that some feelings are bad or scary or should be avoided is what actually does damage.

Brock (and Kelsey) didn't dismiss any concern Dancin might have had during this time. They didn't tell Dancin "don't worry" and then continue in the same pattern. Instead, they allowed her to see Brock in the struggle, they labeled the struggle for what it was, and then they took appropriate steps to find resolve. For a parent, that is the superpower.

Dilemma

"So, how many of you have consistent issues with anxiety?"

I couldn't count all of the hands that shot up—it looked like just about one hand for every kid in the place. As a speaker, I was hoping that the youth leaders in the auditorium were taking note, and that what they noticed would lead them to taking steps in making their youth groups safer and more healing places. Or, at the very least, that they'd check in with their students and work to get them help.

I'm a youth pastor who has cultivated relationships with counselors, spiritual directors, police officers, teachers, principals, headmasters, and parents. All of us are collaborating to create environments where kids can not only find peace, but live the lives they were meant to live. In today's world, passive youth work, just like passive parenting, won't make a dent. And "Lone Ranger" youth ministry, which I will touch on later, just won't cut it these days.

In the past, American kids just kind of grew up and eventually became healthy, contributing adult citizens. A Judeo-Christian mindset pervaded, and many families in those past decades were involved in church and semi-active with their faith. This is no longer the case. In fact, we learned in Chap Clark's book *Hurt* some fifteen years ago that the systems that were originally in place to nurture children and their development have turned in on themselves. The culture moved from being kid centered to being about the adults in charge. This has left our children out in the cold to grow up with an overwhelming sense of abandonment.[1] They are on their own to navigate today's world, and this is having a harmful impact. (Oh, and while we're at it, let's give them each a cell phone. That's a good idea.)

A few years ago, I watched the documentary *The Social Dilemma*. It's a film every youth worker and parent should see. *The Social Dilemma* was made by some of the people who were at the forefront of creating and expanding social media platforms like Facebook and Instagram. What these people realized is that kids on their platforms were suffering in ways that they never would have predicted when they first came up with the technology.

The film shares some alarming stats:

- Self-harm rates are up 62% among 15- to 18-year-old girls compared to 2010.
- Self-harm rates are up 189% for preteen girls compared to 2010.
- Suicide is up 70% among 15- to 18-year-old girls compared to 2010.
- Suicide rates among preteen children are up 151% compared to 2010.[2]

Holy heck! What happened in 2010 to cause all of this?

Well, the film tells us that was the year when about five million more teenagers than ever before received a smartphone for the very first time. In 2010, millions of teenagers began scrolling all day, comparing their lives to others on social media. They began receiving immediate feedback, both good and awful, on their own posts. We can link the mental health of a generation of teenagers to literally one thing: social media. It's pretty incredible to have this kind of evidence.

In the past, laws and regulations protected children from many things. There were rules prohibiting showing cigarette commercials on TV between 8:00 a.m. and noon on Saturday mornings because that's when children would be watching cartoons. These older types of protections do little to protect today's kids. There is a law in most states that you have to be at least eighteen years old to go into a strip club. But with a smartphone, kids can see things that would make a strip club look like a women's prayer meeting. Well, not exactly a women's prayer meeting, but maybe a men's prayer meeting. Basically, what our kids can easily access online is way worse than what they'd experience by actually being at a strip club. The virtual world is a dangerous place. And it's incredibly addicting.

Recently my wife and I were on a winter retreat with our youth group. The theme was all about the Holy Spirit: who the Holy Spirit is, what the Holy Spirit does, and how we can live a life daily empowered by the Holy Spirit. One of our sixth grade girls pulled my wife and me aside and with great emotion confessed to us about her addiction to pornography. This was an eleven-year-old girl. She felt disqualified, dirty, and too filthy to open her life to God's Spirit. She told us that her older cousins had shown her some stuff and she was hooked immediately.

It isn't just pornography that's addicting. The tech industry makes all of their products addicting. Of course they do! Their goal is to see how much of your time—your life—they can get you to give them. Not only do they want your time, they want your attention. Devices and apps are designed to continuously draw us in. This is because something is physically happening in our bodies during these interactions: You post something and then your phone dings and gives you a notification, then dopamine is released in your brain and it's like having a little high. And you can get addicted to any activity that increases your dopamine levels.[3] Consciously or subconsciously, you might wonder what you can do to get another like or another comment. Before you know it, five hours have gone by.

Not long ago I was talking with a group of teenagers about how many hours they spend on social media each day. After they speculated for a while I said that they could actually look this up on their phones. One high school guy said, "I spend maybe a couple of hours at most on Instagram per day." But he looked at his phone to see how long he'd been on there and it told him that he averaged *seven* hours per day. He was stunned!

I wasn't.

These habits we've developed have changed us immensely. But those changes have happened gradually, so that over the last twenty years we haven't really noticed how different our daily lives are. This is evolution: slow, subtle shifts.

THE ANXIOUS TEEN

At this point I can hardly remember a time when I didn't have Facebook or Instagram or Twitter or any of my phone's helpful apps. I mean, what did we do when we were driving? Stop and ask someone for directions? That's ridiculous!

One of the most alarming things shared in *The Social Dilemma* is the fact that every single thing that we do online is being tracked—even little things like how long we pause to look at any given photo. The filmmakers explain that they know everything:
when you're lonely.
when you're horny.
when you go look at an ex-romantic partner.[4]

They track it all.

Social media companies have more information about us than has ever been gathered in human history—more than anyone even imagined could be gathered. We are pouring data into these programs every second we spend online.

What do these companies do with all of this data? Well, they build models that predict our actions so that they can sell us stuff. And whoever has the best model wins. What does the winner get? More participants to sell to advertisers. See, we are the product being sold.

All of the clicks that you've ever clicked have been recorded. And with those clicks these companies use modeling to predict what videos or pictures will keep you engaged and what advertising will get your attention. This is the world our kids are growing up in.

So why would looking at a screen cause so much suffering in the lives of teenagers today?

1. COMPARISON
Teenagers who have issues with depression and with suicidal thoughts report using social media almost constantly: "One-third of teens with depression reported almost constant social media use, as compared to 18

percent of teens who did not have depressive symptoms," according to a Newport Academy article that cites data from a 2021 Common Sense Media report.[5] What is even more alarming is that the report shows that if a teen had struggled with depression, their symptoms actually got worse after being on social media.

Last summer our youth ministry took our students to camp. It felt so good being able to get kids away after the pandemic had let up a bit. One of the first things we did was ask them to put their phones away. The kids who actually did this told us later how much more present they were and how meaningful it was to experience peace. Of course they were.

Kids go online, which leads to them to comparing their lives to each other's, which breeds discontentment and then depression. The data referenced in the Newport Academy article lines up with what I'm seeing in our students: the more severe their symptoms are, the more anxious, lonely, and depressed they feel after using social media.

2. ADDICTION

Kids have a difficult time not overusing online media. Heck, *I* have a hard time not picking up my phone every five minutes. I drive myself nuts at times.

Heavy video gamers are at risk for Internet gaming disorder. Yes—that's an actual disorder. The five most frequently reported issues with this disorder are depression, Internet addiction, anxiety, impulsiveness, and attention-deficit hyperactivity disorder.[6]

Those who are frequently online are susceptible to finding themselves less interested in real life experiences and real-life relationships. Ever seen a group of kids walking in a pack, all looking down at their phones? Or even better, have you ever seen a family out to dinner—and every member is looking at their own screen? It seems like teens take a lot of the flak for phone overuse, but older generations are guilty of this as well—plus we're the ones who invented the technology and gave the phones to the kids in the first place. Still, parents are infuriated by the fact that little Johnny would rather play Minecraft than go outside with his friends or ride his bike. Today's kids spend most of their free time online, and they are showing less interest in leaving the house and hanging out with their friends. And when they are with friends, they are often all sitting together looking at their phones and not interacting much.

Yesterday I was at a party from some folks in our church. A bunch of students were hanging out in the backyard shed. When I abruptly opened the door and yelled to be funny and scare them, not a single one of them flinched. They were sitting on the floor in a circle, each quietly looking at their individual phones. I laughed and said, "Okay, everyone come out with your hands in the air." They laughed…but then went back to their quiet phone staring.

3. CYBERBULLYING
Cyberbullying is a growing problem. Yes, random people can comment on students' pictures or send them incredibly mean messages, but many times the bullying will come not from strangers but from so-called friends their own age.

Recently a student told me she couldn't come to youth group anymore. I asked her what was going on and she said that people from school and even our youth group were bullying her online. I checked into it and she was right. I couldn't believe the comments these kids were making about her. And she was correct, some of it was coming from kids in our youth group. Not core kids, but still. I immediately changed my talk for that evening and dealt with it delicately but head-on. Fortunately I got the girl to come to youth group and afterward she told me that the night was healing for her. YES! A win! But wins are hard to come by in this environment.

4. SLEEP PROBLEMS
Studies are clear that teens consume media at an exponentially higher rate when they have their phone in their bedroom at night. If you factor in impact of the exposure to light (particularly blue light) and the constantly-updated content and the compulsion to see if they got any likes or comments, it's easy to see how teens with phones in their rooms experience delayed and disrupted sleep, which can have a negative effect on school.

Kids in their teen years actually need more sleep than younger children,[7] yet teens today are getting less sleep than ever.

I led a mission trip in Haiti a few years ago and the tensions there were high. The Haitian people were waiting in line to receive health care and food and some clothing from the mission organization we were working with. A few fights broke out while they were waiting and it just felt really unsafe. There was a strange feeling in the air. Haiti can be a pretty volatile place at times—desperation will do that to you. I asked the Haitian ministers what they thought was behind all of the unrest. Shockingly they said they thought it was sleep deprivation. Sleep deprivation? Really? They explained that most Haitians live in homes with no glass in the windows, and residences are really close together in the cities. Everyone has animals and there are trucks with loud engines zooming around all night. Sometimes singing and wailing goes on into all hours. Between the dogs barking, the trucks rumbling by, and noisy neighbors, people do not sleep soundly...ever.

It's amazing to think about how here at home we are choosing poor sleep just so we can have our phones by our side.

5. RISKY BEHAVIORS

Recently a student at youth group came up to me at the end of the night. He was having a difficult time breathing, clearly panicked. "What's going on, man?" I asked. He could hardly speak.

"Brock...a few years ago my girlfriend at the time asked me to send her a picture of my, ya know, my um, private thing."

His embarrassment was palpable.

"Yeah, man. So talk to me, brother."

"Well," he went on, "somebody found it and now it's being passed all over the school on Insta."

"Oh man!"

THE ANXIOUS TEEN

The humiliation was heartbreaking and it was all based on something this kid had done years before. If it weren't for the technology, this never would have happened to him.

Did you know that about 12% of kids between the ages of ten and nineteen have sent a sexual photo to someone?[8] That means that if you have 100 kids in your youth group, twelve of them have probably done that. It's vital they know that these pictures do not just go away. These pictures are owned by whatever platform they're being posted to or sent through. Another risk is that sex offenders may use social networking, chat rooms, email, and online games to contact and exploit children. A fourteen-year-old boy in our youth group gave his testimony, part of which was about how a man (who he thought was another kid) tried to get him to meet up at a park. Thank God his mom was paying attention and discovered what was going on.

This is the world we're in. We are living online. It's what David Kinnaman calls the "Digital Babylon."[9] There are even churches hiring online-specific pastors who do their ministry all in the digital space. These churches don't think people will come back to a physical building. Some youth pastors don't tell kids to put away their phones on retreats. Instead, they ask students to use them to look at their Bible app, take notes, or look things up during their talks. I can see the merit in this approach, but I wonder if it's really the best and healthiest way forward.

Other youth workers are going the opposite direction. They are confiscating kids' phones or asking them to put their phones in a box on the way into the youth room. They are looking at the data and research on technology and social media and mental health and giving it to parents, asking adults to hold off as long as possible before getting their child a phone. I see the merit in that as well, plus some limitations.

I wonder if we could have a both/and approach to this dilemma of social media and the constant use of devices. I like both/and approaches when it comes to difficult topics.

As a youth pastor I've thought a lot about this.

What if we asked our young people to join us in a challenge where—together—we fasted from our phones, gaming, and social media? What if we also showed kids how to use their phones responsibly?

What if we asked them to read Scriptures from their Bible app and also taught them how to use their physical Bible and journal for a few minutes a day?

What if Mom and Dad were encouraged to wait as long as possible to put a device in their kids' hands, but when they did they were supported and educated on how to do so with thoughtful care?

What if we looked reality squarely in the eye and found a new way forward?

SHIFTING AWAY FROM A "LONE RANGER" MENTALITY

As I mentioned earlier, we have to reject the "Lone Ranger" mentality when it comes to both ministry and parenting. Lone Rangers think they can go it alone. Thinking that I can and should pastor or parent alone, specifically because no one else could do it better, is a common belief today.

For a long time, my Lone Ranger mentality told me that I was "it" for kids. I felt like I was the one who needed to solve all of their problems, change their minds and thinking, be their rock in times of difficulty, and be their source of spiritual experience.

Me, myself, and I. Not even my well-trained leaders quite measured up, and in my mind, parents certainly did not get it.

This mentality leads to troubling theological dysfunction. My wife lovingly and sarcastically calls this out when she sees it in me. It's what we can also call a Jesus Christ complex.

Early on (I was young, friends) I believed that parents should just get out of the way and let me take over when their children got to middle school. I was the authority on raising healthy and whole teenagers, and I would hand them back at eighteen ready to launch into adulthood. Over the years, with blessed maturity, that mentality morphed into a more benign sense of my own importance and responsibility in the lives of these kids, one that would eat at me, costing me sleep. As a parent, it is not so different. I often feel this sense of sole responsibility in both roles. Some of it stems from a place of real caring, but I know the rest comes out of fear and my propensity to hold onto control. How bogus is that?!

I remember speaking at Glendale Presbyterian Church when I was about twenty-three. I was the junior high director and Chap Clark was my boss. As I was speaking I made an off-the-cuff comment about parents being the problem. I laughed—and at that exact moment caught eyes with Chap. Chap had no smile on his face and was shaking his head, "No." Ugh, I knew I'd said the wrong thing.

I've learned better since then, but this is a common mindset in youth ministry. Don't believe me that youth workers think this way? Just yesterday I was on a youth worker Facebook group. You might think that these groups would be fun, light, helpful, and encouraging, but most of what I've found there is a big fat helping of petty, ignorant, and judgey comments, with maybe a tiny hint of encouragement on the side.

The debate yesterday was over this exact topic: *Should parents be involved at youth group?* The crazy thing is, most of the youth workers still believed that Mom and Dad should just get out of the way. I was amazed at their short-sightedness, but based on my own journey, not completely surprised. Fortunately, older youth workers were chiming in with some wise perspectives.

When youth workers have a Lone Ranger/Jesus Christ complex, they sometimes even feel threatened by other adults, beyond the parents, who are being helpful and in the lives of students. I've actually heard youth workers imply that students don't need a counselor because, well, they have their youth worker. "They don't need a coach, I'll coach them." "They don't need other pastors, I'll be the one to pastor them." "Mom and Dad, I got this. We don't need you much anymore."

This Lone Ranger thinking flies in the face of all the research being done right now on young people and faith. That research is clear: Kids need multiple adults in their lives. Maybe this should be our first priority as youth workers: Get a bunch of adults with different skill sets committed to each one of our students.

Today, I'm all about being partners. I prioritize building partnerships with parents, counselors, teachers, spiritual directors, addiction specialists, coaches, principals, and anyone who cares about kids. We are a network of passionate adults who absolutely care about our students' hearts, minds, and souls! Many of these adults love Jesus, some do not, but we all are in the deep end trying to create pathways of healing for kids. And man, I've got to tell you, it's way better being on a team than operating as an individual. (I think even the Bible says something about that. Something about a cord of three strands not quickly broken. Yeah, I think that's in the Bible. If it isn't, it should be.)

Are you stuck in a Lone Ranger mentality? Here are some questions to ask yourself:

- Do you have healthy patterns and set healthy boundaries for yourself?
- How much do you seek affirmation from others?
- How important do you see yourself as being in the lives of your students compared with parents, teachers, other pastors, etc.?
- How do you react to criticism?
- Do you become jealous when a student brags about the impact of their small group leader, coach, or teacher?

CHAPTER TAKEAWAYS

- Social media and smartphone usage have a negative impact on mental health.
- It's possible to take a both/and approach to social media. Consider taking on a challenge alongside your students where you all practice fasting from phones, gaming, and social media for a period of time, then talk collectively about your experiences. What did you learn? How did it affect your life? Did it change how you saw yourself and others?

THE ANXIOUS TEEN

- We as youth workers need to build partnerships with the other trusted adults in the lives of today's kids: parents, teachers, coaches, counselors, fellow youth workers, etc. A Lone Ranger mentality won't take us where we want to go.

NOTES *from a Mental Health Therapist*

Have you ever been out to a restaurant and noticed how many times you catch a group of people sharing the same table all on their phones? Recently I was out to eat and watched a woman with someone I presumed was her son. He was dressed in his baseball uniform and they were eating lunch, each of them on their phone the whole time.

This made me sad. What a missed opportunity to connect with your kid! And here's the thing: This situation isn't unusual.

I hear all the time from parents who can't keep their kids off their phones. They struggle with kids bringing phones to their rooms at night, or being on them during dinner (if they have dinner as a family). The challenge with teens having their phone after "bedtime" is that they are still connected to the world. Just like the teenager Brock mentioned who was on his phone for seven hours without realizing it. The hours after parents go to sleep are prime for overuse. Teens stay up scrolling, texting, and chatting until the early morning.

I am an advocate of being aware of what kids are doing online. I also strongly encourage parents to be aware of the ways teens are trying to hide their online activity, but to do so through open communication and straightforward questions, from a place of genuine curiosity and interest.

I know many parents believe that reading their teen's diary is a good idea. They believe they can learn how their kid is doing, discover if they are struggling with anything their parents don't know about, and generally keep tabs on their kid's emotional health. I agree that on the surface these are good instincts on the parents' part—but I believe that open conversation addresses these same concerns in a more appropriate and healthy way. We can apply this to teens' online activity too.

Many parents reach out to youth leaders when they learn about their kid's online presence. This can get complicated quickly. Chaos can ensue when a parent reaches out to the youth leader to tell them they've been online and just read that their kid wishes they could die. And when a parent comes to a youth leader saying, "My kids hates me. What do I do?"

Remember that you as the youth leader do not need to be pulled into the chaos. Recognize the teen you are discussing and remind yourself what you know about them.

This is when you can rely on the team that you have built up. Reach out to a therapist to talk about what happens next. Be aware of trends in technology and what websites are all the rage today, and pay attention to any updates from law enforcement about related risks. Look for ways to bring more healthy, loving adults into teenagers' lives, and to partner with parents as they look to set healthy boundaries about technology and social media with their kids.

Knowing Where We've Been to Navigate Where We're Going

My wife, Kelsey, and I had just finished meeting with one of our seventh grade girls. She had literally just finished sixth grade two weeks ago—she was barely twelve years old. And she was already really struggling, like so many others. We met with her after seeing that she'd posted a TikTok of herself weeping as she had what could only be described as a panic attack. This video caused us to immediately jump into action. We set up a time with her to find out how we could help. And then, just a few hours before we were supposed to meet with her, she posted another video, this time of herself making out with another seventh grade girl.

This isn't at all what I imagined my future would look like when I first began this youth worker journey so long ago.

I was a college sophomore back in 1991 when I began my youth ministry career. I saw myself doing youth ministry for the rest of my life. You know, eating pizza, playing games, singing songs with hand motions, and then giving students a little Jesus before sending them on their way.

Oh, don't be mistaken. I took it very seriously. Youth culture has always been complex. But the struggles weren't anything new, ya know? Kids in the '90s were pretty much like I had been when I was their age, albeit with some minor differences.

Instead of playing an Atari, they were playing Super Nintendo.
Instead of having a mullet like John Stamos, they were shaving their heads like Sublime.

THE ANXIOUS TEEN

Instead of listening to Poison, they were listening to Pearl Jam.
Instead of being horny, oh wait, yeah, that was the same.

But at that time, kids were basically just like the kids of every generation before them. Or at least that was the thinking. Kids will be kids, right? Of course, I wasn't stupid. I figured that there would be minor method changes and adaptations throughout my time in ministry. Nothing major, though. There's nothing new under the sun, right? For goodness' sakes, that's in the Bible.

In my first years, youth ministry just didn't seem very difficult. It was perfect for my temperament. It was super fun, and even the hard and the difficult parts were fulfilling. Back then I couldn't have begun to imagine doing what is required today of youth workers in this kind of world, with these kinds of kids and these kinds of struggles.

Growing up, I was kind of a misfit. I was diagnosed with a learning disability in fourth grade and school just didn't come naturally to me. As a result, I focused on two things: being funny and being athletic. That's where I'd make my mark! Those two things did come naturally. But because those were the only two things I believed I was good at, it was actually pretty limiting. I completely avoided thoughts about the future. As the class clown I couldn't imagine being an adult. I couldn't imagine going to work and paying bills. I entered college as a P.E. major, because at least that way I could play dodgeball for the rest of my life.

During my freshman year of college, God got a hold of my life in a very real and unexpected way. I was being discipled by one of my professors and he said I'd make a great youth pastor. It's important to emphasize that he didn't say this nonchalantly or even merely suggest it. It was more of a directive, like, "Brock, this is what you should do with your life."

And when he said this, it rang true. Honestly, it more than rang true. It was like hearing the voice of God. I immediately saw my future, which I had never been able to picture before. I could see myself doing important things. Not that dodgeball wasn't important. But I could see myself investing in the next generation. It felt like I knew what I was supposed to do for the rest of my life.

And in the early '90s, I understood exactly what that meant: I'd create an environment where kids felt cared for, we'd lead some games, and then I'd tell funny stories that would, somehow, unexpectedly, lead them to Jesus. So I followed the path toward becoming a youth pastor. I jumped in with both feet. It just felt so natural.

Through the 1990s and early 2000s, everything I touched exploded with numerical growth, which was how we rated success back in those days. My first full-time job was as the junior high director at a Presbyterian church in Southern California. When I started there we had about five seventh and eighth graders. Within six months, we were running after school basketball and boxing programs, and when we threw our monthly Friday night activity, no joke, at least 2,000 kids from across the city would show up to our church gymnasium. And that was just seventh and eighth grade kids. It was absolutely insane.

Every week we were leading kids to Jesus. But as the years went on, things began to change. In fact, I began to change. The problems students were experiencing became more and more complex, and I was becoming very serious about my life's calling to young people. I wanted to be effective. I wanted to be professional. I wanted to make a difference. If kids were changing, and I wanted to be more effective, I needed to make some serious shifts. I needed to adapt or I needed to move on. But even at that point I had no idea how much more the world would change. I couldn't imagine back then that only serious and professional adults would be capable of doing effective youth work as we moved into the future.

As a youth pastor, I began seeing new struggles that were slowly emerging with each new crop of students.

This generation—those born between 1997 and 2012—are called Generation Z, Post-Millennials, or the iGeneration, and they are unique. We'll look more at them in a minute.

My generation, Generation X, is made up of people born between 1965 and 1980. We are also known as the forgotten generation or latchkey kids because we were the first generation to either have only one parent living with us or come home after school to an empty house because both of our parents were working. Generation X is the first generation that has NOT done as well financially as their parents did. We lived through Watergate, the energy crisis, Y2K, activism, corporate downsizing, AIDS, the end of the Cold War, and a rapidly increased divorce rate.

Church leaders in the late '90s and early 2000s talked a lot about Generation X and how to reengage this angry and disenfranchised generation that was pulling away from organized religion, especially the Christian church. If you want to see how angry Generation X was, just watch the documentary *Woodstock 99*, directed by Garret Price. It captures some essential characteristics of the dark edge of our generation. We listened to music like Pearl Jam, Nirvana, Rage Against the Machine, Dr. Dre, Snoop Dogg, and Soundgarden. Aside from music, many of those in Generation X were shaped by having to take care of themselves from a young age since their parents were working, as well as by watching their politicians lie and their jobs disappear during a financial crisis. Being a young youth pastor during these years, there were certain songs we had to stop playing during worship because a mosh pit would break out. Ha! It was absolutely ridiculous.

Parenting Gen X kids was kind of a hands-off deal. "Kids will be kids" was the motto, and it helped parents deal with the guilt of not being around as much as their parents had been.

As Generation X moved through its teenage years, society's fear of what would happen if kids were bored peaked. Boredom was the enemy because, as we all know, busy kids stay out of trouble. Right? In response, youth ministry began to shift to a heavy program model. We had to if we wanted to keep kids off the streets and prevent them from being bored and getting into trouble in the neighborhood.

When I first became a youth pastor in the early '90s, we had morning Sunday school and then Wednesday night youth group, plus a monthly activity. By the time 1995 hit we were running daily basketball and boxing Monday through Saturday, Sunday school programs, weekend activities, and of course our Wednesday night youth group. Dude, that's seven days a week, and that is what is called an insane schedule. But again, in response to that generation's needs, parenting struggles, and larger societal fears, that made sense. Keep those Gen X kids busy, brother!

Millennials are people born roughly between 1981 and 1995. Some of the heroes of their coming-of-age years include Ashton Kutcher and Serena Williams. As teens, they listened to singers like Britney Spears and Christina Aguilera, with some boy bands like 'N Sync and Backstreet Boys thrown in. During this same era, rap music also went mainstream and was taking over the airwaves.

In about 2004 our ministry brought in a hard rock band called Stavesacre that Generation X would have really loved. But our youth group was now full of millennials. Most of the kids walked out and hung out in the church's courtyard during the show. They just weren't into that kind of loud music anymore, and it seemed scary to them. I mean, Stavesacre didn't do choreographed dance moves while belting out their lyrics. Ha! Millennial kids are the product of parents choosing to have fewer children beginning later in life, and so as they grew up they were seen as a precious commodity to protect. In a safer world than we have ever lived in, millennial kids were monitored and supervised beyond anything the previous generations had experienced.

Physical safety was the priority for parents of millennials. They were the first generation required by law to sit in car seats and wear seat belts. They grew up in a pre-9/11, child-focused world, and they saw the birth of small, handheld cellular phones. Many millennials grew up as children of divorce, but they hoped to be the generation to turn things around in the world.

Millennials were the first generation of young adults who walked around with cell phones in their hands telling them what was going on in the world. And they cared deeply about what was happening—but not as much as getting into an amazing college. So while church influence declined, education's influence rose. Millennial kids and their parents began to fear that millennials wouldn't get into prestigious colleges, which would be devastating. In response, millennials took up activity after activity, and resumé-building became a high priority. Youth pastors began to see anxiety levels rise among kids, and for the first time we youth workers regularly complained about students being too busy for church and youth group. By

THE ANXIOUS TEEN

2010, a post-Christian culture was in full swing. Society was now looking outside the church for help in raising their kids.

Parents began to take control of this resumé-building, signing up their kids for multiple sports during the same season, plus SAT and ACT tutoring. Parents took on the role of taxi drivers, chauffeuring their kids from activity to activity, meeting to meeting, and team to team.

And then, something new emerged. As this next generation came of age in the early- to mid-2000s, we became aware of all the pressure they were feeling, the result of a culture that had pushed them to be successful at literally everything. Kids felt abandoned and were carrying hurt like we hadn't seen in a long while. If you're not sure about all of this, just read Chap Clark's groundbreaking book, *Hurt 2.0*.[10]

Through this period, the focus narrowed on the adults in charge of all of the activities youth participated in, and certain results were expected. Sports were no longer about building character, but about winning—if the coach wanted to keep their job. School was no longer about learning but about test scores and job security for teachers and principals—and, of course, about all of the money associated with those test scores.

For the first time, youth pastors began to notice that they were out of their depth. Our programs were no longer resonating. What I did in the early '90s—pizza, games, songs with hand motions, a funny talk that subtly pointed them to Jesus—wasn't nearly as effective. Youth pastors worth their salt were now having to partner with counseling centers and professionals who understood how to help kids who were self-harming in response to all of the pressure and hurt they were facing. Youth pastors who took this seriously began to go deeper in their teaching, going beneath the surface level to discuss things like suffering, why God allows hard things to happen, and the big questions of life. Youth workers who understood what was happening and succeeded at meeting young people's needs began creating sanctuary at church, and ministered with an awareness of where students were.

But where students were continued to change and shift. Around 2012 it became clear that kids weren't just carrying hurt, they were experiencing a lot more. In youth ministry we began hearing about kids having regular panic attacks. We couldn't get kids away from their phones, and social media was beginning to take over their lives. And this leads us to the next two generations: Generation Z and, coming right behind them, Generation Alpha.

These are the kids we in youth ministry are working with now. Generation Z is made up of people born between 1997 and 2010. Generation Alpha are those born after 2010. That means the sixth graders you have in 2022 are Generation Alpha. These generations have their own unique challenges, and they are who this book will focus on.

Many confuse these younger generations with millennials, especially the Gen-Zers, but just like in previous generations, new things are emerging and so must our methods and understandings. If we're going to come alongside them and better minister to them and equip them to follow Jesus in this not-so-easy world, we've got to look below the surface to see what is really going on in the hearts and minds of these precious ones.

Gen Z is known for being technologically adept to the point of becoming addicted. They're also known for being politically active, evidenced through actions like organized walk-outs and BLM marches.

Many experts say that Gen Z and Gen Alpha will be a lot alike, but time will tell. I think Generation Alpha could be a generation that not only grows up in a politically divided nation in the U.S. but also lives with what our broken systems are creating: anger, fear, misinformation, mistrust, hatred, and demonization of the other.

Gen Alpha will also grow up in a world where gender and sexual fluidity are more fully taught and embraced. Whether you are for this, completely against this, or somewhere in between, the topic of gender identity will profoundly impact conversation and thinking in the coming years. This could end up being the straw that breaks the camel's back for conservatives. My bet is that private schools and homeschooling will continue to explode with growth. This is already happening, but the trend will be compounded.

THE ANXIOUS TEEN

Both Gen Z and Gen Alpha are being raised in a world with high pressure, high expectations, and high levels of anxiety. Airport security and school lockdown drills are their norm. Both generations are blessed and cursed with the nearly infinite tools that come with today's technology.

It's also important to note that these generations, just like their elder siblings, struggle with a lack of quality free time. In fact, Gen Alpha has significantly less playtime, on average, than their millennial parents enjoyed when they were growing up.[11] This might not seem like a big deal, but the lack of quality free time profoundly affects health, mental wellness, socialization, and even children's cognitive ability.[12]

For those of us who have been in the day-to-day grind of youth ministry for over thirty years, what we're seeing now with Gen Z and Gen Alpha is not necessarily what we expected. The changes can seem daunting, but the truth is that it's *because* of those unexpected twists and turns that we are still in ministry. We can't leave! Too much has happened and there's too much at stake for us to bow out now.

In my book *Youth Ministry 2027*, I wrote about a coming movement. A cultural mass movement born out of desperation and a shift toward the only one who could give us peace. In the late 1960s and into the early 1970s, people were in a place of utter desperation. There were riots in the streets. This was in the midst of the anti-war movement and the civil rights movement and the backlash of it all. This violence in the streets became almost the norm. It felt scary, like *Left Behind* was happening before the books were even written. People of influence were being assassinated, young men were fighting in the Vietnam War, teenagers were in the streets picketing against that very war, and everyone was feeling it. It felt like the world was coming to an end. Even young people's music heroes—Janis Joplin, Jimi Hendrix, and others—were dying from drug overdoses. Every week something new and awful would be reported on the nightly news. There was a desperation in the air. By the early 1970s, there was a response: a movement was emerging. A movement toward Jesus. Within just a few years, millions of teenagers had given their lives to Jesus. That's right: millions. Think about that.

I want you to fully understand what that time would have been like. Imagine going on a youth retreat in the middle of all of that unfolding brokenness. Picture yourself there, in the midst of everything these kids are carrying. Imagine that you all sense something emerging there on that retreat. Strangely, there seems to be a sense of hope. God seems to be doing something, something different, something new and deep. You can see this, right? There you are, with your cool hippie hair, and something is happening in your midst.

And here's the amazing thing: When you go home at the end of that retreat, it doesn't feel like anything ends. In fact, it REALLY doesn't end. The retreat was just the beginning. Your kids are starting prayer meetings at their schools and are sharing their faith. Before long, entire schools and communities are coming to faith. Everyone has collectively felt the desperation and the brokenness of the world and it has caused a whole school, a whole city, a whole region and state and eventually the whole country to be open to what God is doing.

This was the Jesus movement of the 1970s.

And this—somewhere like it, anyway—is where I believe we will be again soon. It's one of the reasons why there's no way in heck I'm getting out of youth ministry. Even though it's so different from what I once thought it was. Even though I'm connecting with students in the midst of harder struggles than I ever imagined. There is so much potential for a life-changing, Jesus-filled movement. What we need to do now is not back away, but to understand the moment. How is all of this playing out in the lives of our kids? What is going on in the hearts and minds and souls of the teenagers we've been called to? If we don't ask these questions, we just might miss this cultural moment and all of its beautiful potential.

CHAPTER TAKEAWAYS

- Gen Z and Gen Alpha are being raised in a world with high pressure, high expectations, and high levels of anxiety, as well as a lack of quality free time.

- Many of the challenges in youth work today are different from those that existed in the past, because in many ways students and their struggles are different than they once were. We need to understand the moment we're in and meet kids where they are in it—not back away.

NOTES *from a Mental Health Therapist*

Are today's students truly more complex than students were in the past? I wonder if students aren't becoming more complex, but the world we live in is—more complicated, and bigger than it used to be. With social media, instant access to world news, and instant access to people's lives, we are certainly more connected, more informed, and sometimes more overwhelmed than ever before.

Adolescence is when teens begin to get space from adults. They want to be independent. They want to push boundaries.

Because teens are pushing for independence they begin to identify more with their peers than their parents. At that stage of life, it becomes easier to be understood by someone on their own level. It feels so much better to have a conversation with someone you feel understands you rather than to be talked at by an adult.

In his book *Brainstorm*,[13] Dr. Dan Siegel—a psychiatrist and one of the leading experts in the study of the brain—explains four features of brain growth that happen in adolescence:

Novelty seeking emerges: an increased drive for rewards that creates the inner motivation to try new things. This creates more risk taking.

Social engagement: enhanced peer connection and new friendships.

Increased emotional intensity: This could mean that emotions rule teenagers' lives for a period.

Creative exploration: teens have an expanded sense of consciousness. This means they can access some abstract thinking, allowing them to question the status quo.

Knowing Where We've Been to Navigate Where We're Going

Siegel actually suggests that to maintain vitality in our adult lives, we need to hold onto these adolescent traits.

With all of that in mind, I think the best way to continue connecting with and impacting teens is to be flexible. We need to be open to listening and watching. We need to step outside of ourselves and hear young people's needs. As youth leaders, doing this well means holding onto the young parts of ourselves. Maintaining some of the essence of adolescence—questioning things as they are, remaining creative and curious, taking some risks, being open to emotions and new things—will help us as adults stay connected to the young people we care about.

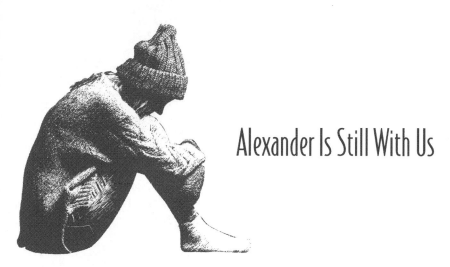

Alexander Is Still With Us

I was sitting next to my friend Michael Boring one morning in our college chapel service. I went to a conservative Christian college in Eastern Tennessee and we had to attend chapel services four times a week. Yeah, you read that right. And not only was my friend's last name Boring, and not only did every student have to attend those boring chapel services, we also had to take Bible classes and be involved in local churches, plus be involved in ministry. It was total immersion. It was a lot, but I actually thrived during those years.

Back to that morning: I was sitting next to Michael when I noticed that a portion of his Bible had been stapled shut.

"Dude, what in the world?" I whispered to him.

"Yeah," he said. "I'm stapling the book Song of Songs shut until I get married."

"Huh??" What was in that book?!

As soon as that chapel service was over I went to my dorm room and opened that bad boy up to see what all of the fuss was.

This erotic little Bible book is about two lovers, and it doesn't ease you into it like a good Christian book should. It doesn't begin like, "We were sitting on a park bench listening to Amy Grant and telling each other our prayer requests."

THE ANXIOUS TEEN

NO! It begins by saying, "Your lovemaking is intoxicating like wine."

Insane, man! Boy, do I love the Bible!

That's not the last time I spent with Song of Songs. I later interned for a year at Denton Bible Church. The pastor there, Tom Nelson, is famous for his great work on the Song of Songs, and his teaching never quite left me. Over the years I'd go back to the Song of Songs for wisdom, marital inspiration, and for additional names to call Kelsey's breasts. One passage that I've never been able to shake is in the very first chapter:

> (Woman speaking)
> "Do not stare at me because I am dark, because I am darkened by the sun. My mother's sons were angry with me and made me take care of the vineyards; my own vineyard I had to neglect."
> —Song of Songs 1:6

So this woman is insecure about something. She's been working in the field and she's self-conscious about the color of her skin. Her culture had told her what was ideal, and she was not measuring up.

It might be difficult for some of us to fully understand this, especially those of us who are white. I remember pouring baby oil on my skin in the '80s, lying out in the sun trying to get darker. Many of us look at tan skin and we think the opposite of what this girl's culture told her. In her culture, and in certain cultures today, this was something she learned to be embarrassed about.

And so she says, "Please do not look at me too closely." Her insecurity is speaking loudly.

This is something most of our teens can relate to in their own ways. Just a few weeks ago a girl came up to me right after youth group. Recently her parents had gotten divorced and there has been all kinds of turmoil for their family. She confessed to me that she needed help because she had stopped eating. I had noticed that she had lost weight, but of course I hadn't said anything. She said that she had begun binging and purging and that it was really scaring her. We immediately got her help and she's in the process of finding wholeness. But what she was going through is unfortunately pretty common in our world, where there's an ideal standard that no one can measure up to, including the Photoshopped models on Instagram.

In our world, people judge and value each other based on appearances. This is not new, though social media has heightened the pressure surrounding how we see ourselves. We are still struggling today with something closely related to what's in a three-thousand-year-old poem from Song of Songs. Those ancient words are still relevant. Our culture is not as different from theirs as we might imagine.

What we have is a screwed-up idea of beauty, and a screwed-up idea that beauty is where our value lies. This is what leads girls to post pictures on social media hoping the comments will affirm that they are pretty. And if the comments aren't over-the-top positive, it's time to delete that photo. Many times the comments people make online are awful and degrading. The more I think about it, the more I feel upset and angry. But I don't want to stop with those feelings. So I'm asking myself: How did we get here? What led the woman in Song of Songs to feel this kind of insecurity, and what causes girls and even guys to buy into our ridiculous notions of what beauty is and crave affirmation online?

Obviously (or not…), to find the answer, we've got to go back in history to Alexander the Great.

If you're not especially familiar with Alexander the Great, I'll give you the basics. He lived about 350 years before Jesus came onto the scene. Alexander the Great was Greek and his hope was to conquer the entire world, and then he wanted to give that conquered world a Hellenistic (the term for the culture of ancient Greece) worldview. He wanted Greek thought and Greek perspective and Greek worldview to sweep across the world. He was brutal in his conquering, but brilliant in his wooing of the people he conquered. Alexander would slowly and patiently get conquered groups to embrace his way of seeing the world.

The Greek way of looking at the world during this era is fascinating. As one of their philosophers, Protagoras, said very early on, "Man is the measure of all things."[14]

THE ANXIOUS TEEN

To the Greeks at that time, human beings were the center of the universe, which meant that human thought and wisdom were the highest form of truth.

- Not God's wisdom.
- Not God's truth.
- Humans were the center.

So in that place and time, if you needed to know the answers to some of life's biggest question, you wouldn't look beyond the self. You wouldn't look beyond human wisdom. Sound familiar?

In that time, Alexander would conquer a people group with the intention of eventually compelling them to see all of life through a Greek lens. They would build stadiums in conquered cities for the public display of athletic contests. Temples were built to honor local gods, and festivals were held to celebrate pagan holidays. In the midst of these attractions, the conquered Jewish populations struggled to maintain their worldview. The Greeks were highly strategic in spreading their way of seeing all of life. To the Greek mind, human wisdom and a very particular type of body were to be valued above everything else. We can see this even today when we look at ancient Greek writings and art.

The Greek educational system was remarkably effective at instilling Greek ideals into entire generations of young people. Busts of Greek gods and heroes celebrated the ultimate ideal: the human form. Young Jews were forced to read Homer, Euripides, and Plato, a way of instilling Greek values in these Jews. Jews were taught to draw and sculpt, often creating the forms of Greek gods. They were submersed in Greek thinking. Slowly they, and much of the world, began to accept the Greek ideal.

At its core, Hellenism was humanism, glorifying human beings above all other creatures and portraying a specific type of human body as the ultimate in physical beauty. In that culture, it was believed that truth could be known only through the human mind, and pleasure was the objective of life.

So what happened if you did not measure up to the Greek ideal? At best, you were marginalized. If someone didn't look like the human ideal, well then, just get rid of them. Eventually this idea led to a Roman law that said if a child was born who didn't fit within particular standards you could, legally, throw the baby out with the garbage and leave them to die of exposure.[15]

Greek philosopher Aristotle wrote in *Politics*, "As to the raising and exposure of children, let there be a law that no deformed child shall live."[16]

So what would happen is when a baby was born and it had a birthmark that was displeasing or had some deformity great or small, you'd take it out to the elements and the weather and the wild animals and just leave it. This was the standard. This was the conclusion of Greek thinking in that time.

Now the reason I'm going into all of this history is to say that many years before you or I were here, a notion had already swept across the known world that a specific ideal of beauty should be upheld. And Alexander help lead the whole thing.

> *This is what is beautiful.*
> *Only beautiful people have true worth.*
> *What do we do with the rest?*
> *Get rid of them.*
> *It's like* Hunger Games.
> *It's hell on earth.*

Well, what about today?

Twenty million females and at least ten million males will struggle with eating disorders in their lifetime.[17] Ninety percent of teenagers who have eating disorders today are female, and about 70% of teenage girls state that photographs of models and celebrities in the media motivated their "ideal" body shape.[18]

THE ANXIOUS TEEN

And here is something that really puts this issue into perspective: "Every 62 minutes, at least one person dies as a result of an eating disorder."[19]
Nine billion dollars were spent in 2020 on unnecessary cosmetic surgeries.[20]

Is Greek Hellenistic thinking still with us?

Yesterday my wife and I ate at a restaurant. She pointed out at least five different young women there who'd had their lips done. That was just in one restaurant, during one meal. These young women's lips were evidence that the women didn't feel quite good enough without changing their appearance.

Every time you open Instagram, you are bombarded with filtered and posed images. And these images convey an ideal, again and again. *A man looks like this and a woman looks like this. This is the standard and you don't measure up.*

Is Greek Hellenism alive and well?

You bet.

So back to the passage:

She says, "*Do not stare at me because of my appearance.*"

Three thousand years later, we are still caught up in how we look. The same issue is killing us.

The amazing thing is that we see the complete opposite of this in the upside-down teachings of Jesus. The followers of Jesus took his words seriously and it changed the way they saw themselves and each other.

During the time when it was lawful in Rome to throw babies out to the elements, Christians became known for rescuing and raising these discarded children as their own. Why? Because the way of Jesus compelled them to. They understood that everyone is created in God's image and that all of life is sacred.

Remember how it was in the beginning? Man and woman walking in the garden with God. These two image bearers, naked and unashamed.

- No insecurity.
- No judgment.
- No fear.
- No shame.

See, the gospel is about God bringing us back.
Bringing us back to himself and restoring our worth.

This is what God is longing to do in you and in me. This is what he's longing to do in our young people's lives.

The apostle Paul understood that the gospel spoke directly to the insecurities and brokenness in each of us. Check out his argument in 2 Corinthians 3:18:

> And we all, who with unveiled faces contemplate the Lord's glory,
> are being transformed into his image with ever-increasing glory,
> which comes from the Lord, who is the Spirit.

This image is being restored, giving all of us a growing awareness of our worth, our true value. The gospel is so relevant for the issues our students are going through today, and for us as adults. It's good news for a generation that is struggling with so much. God is bringing us back to himself and restoring us.

CHAPTER TAKEAWAYS

- Distorted ideas around beauty and self-worth have existed for thousands of years.
- Focusing on Christ can change us. We are all created in the image of God. We are all being transformed to be more like God. We are all capable of showing deep love and care for others. Those are the things of true beauty.

THE ANXIOUS TEEN

NOTES *from a Mental Health Therapist*

I received a call the other day from a parent wanting counseling for her daughter. In talking with the mom ahead of time, I learned that her daughter is really smart. As a junior in high school she earned really high grades and was involved in student leadership. She played school sports and held a part-time job. Her parents suggested that she had always been a really happy person, until recently. She seemed to be struggling and was exhibiting signs of disordered eating. Both parents were concerned.

This adolescent girl had absorbed the message, both at home and at school, that she needed to do better, and needed to look better. What she internalized was that she wasn't good enough. This message wasn't actually spoken, but modeled. Despite being told she was loved, being a good student, and being celebrated for her "wins," the words she heard spoken weren't enough to combat the nonverbal messages saying she needed to do better and look better, ideas she was internalizing.

Both her parents followed eating programs. They both were striving for goals, and both wanted to look "better." The curious thing is when asked what "better" meant, they couldn't define it. They were chasing their own rainbow.

Complicating matters with their daughter was the topic of college. It was her junior year and the pressure was on. She was working hard to live up to her parents' standards, both spoken and unspoken. It seems like the legacy of Alexander is alive and well in that household.

It isn't uncommon to learn that teens have "hidden" social media accounts that their parents don't know exist. These are the accounts where they seek validation, learn how to get that validation, and generally pretend to be who they think their parents won't approve of. Another teen I worked with had a hidden account dedicated to eating disorders. She's not the only one. Parents need to become more aware of the things they are unaware of. They need to open the door to conversations about the things they don't want to know.

No parent wants to see their child hurting. No parent wants to believe that what they are doing to "better themselves" is negatively impacting their child. As role models, we need to become aware of the messages we are sending.

This is a huge task because it means we need to be aware of the messages we carry. We need to ask ourselves questions: *What is it that I believe about myself?*

Part of me wishes we could go back and ask Alexander what he believed about himself. Did he really believe he was all that, or did he work to prove it to himself by creating little Alexanders everywhere?

Stress and Anxiety Class

I couldn't believe the sign-ups. Our youth ministry team had decided to offer a class on Sunday mornings called "Anxiety and Stress Relief for Teens." An overwhelming percentage of our kids registered. I already knew that about 32% of teenagers today have been diagnosed with an anxiety disorder.[21] That's a big number—and that's just those who've been diagnosed. To see more than 75% of our kids come to a class on anxiety relief confirmed that we had a major problem on our hands.

Watching all of those students file into the youth room for a class on this topic made our team realize a few things. One was that we needed to make sure our regular youth group times were being programmed with an awareness of where kids are today and the big issues and struggles they face. It's not that we needed to change everything we were doing and make everything we offered contemplative, whispering the whole night so we wouldn't overwhelm our fragile students. It's also not that we couldn't play games or needed to address anxiety each week. It's just that we needed to plan our weekly meetings with an awareness of what kids are dealing with every day. We needed to be more thoughtful and talk about the whole range of things that matter to our kids. We needed to help them understand and navigate what was going on inside of them.

Ashton, one of our ninth grade guys, came to our anxiety relief class. Ashton always seemed to have a smile on his face, and I wouldn't have thought he'd have a need for a class like this. When he arrived, I felt uncomfortable, almost guilty, that I was surprised to see him. His presence was convicting. I knew better to think that only the obvious kids—you know, the ones who are withdrawn or socially uncomfortable, stereotypically anxious—would need this kind of help. Anxiety is an across-the-board epidemic.

We started talking one-on-one, and eventually Ashton told me that school had been stressing him out, building up to some big-time anxiety. "I just haven't been able to shake it," he said. He shared that he thought his anxiety led to him making some bad decisions, hoping that they would help him forget about his problems. It turns out it hadn't actually been his idea to come to the class. "My parents made me come to this thing," he said, smiling.

The research shows the same things most teenagers say: School is the top source of their stress. I sat next to Ashton in the back of the room as Chris Butler, Ph.D.—the counselor and psychologist teaching the class—began.[22] To start, we learned the difference between stress and anxiety. I'd always thought they were basically the same thing. In our class, Butler taught us that chronic and long-term stress can *cause* anxiety, high blood pressure, and a weakened immune system. Stress leads to anxiety. Everyone is affected by stress at one time or another, and the resulting anxiety can be overwhelming. "Gang," the instructor said, "anxiety can also cause you to make really bad choices that can possibly lead you into some serious regret. When we are desperate to escape those anxious feelings and we do not have the skills or know how to deal with them, we'll do anything to get away or to turn our minds off." "Yeah, that's why my parents made me come here this morning!" Ashton leaned over and said to me. "Yeah, me too," I whispered back. We both started laughing out loud and kind of distracted the whole class. I felt like a middle school boy in the back of the room. "Um, sorry."

During the class, we learned how normal anxiety is. Stress, Butler said, is sometimes a good thing. When you have a test coming up, a little stress can cause you to study harder so you do well. The problem is that it can also lead to harmful anxiety, especially when it is irrational or prevents you from being able to focus. Sometimes the anxiety can come between us and our friends, especially when we avoid spending time with them or talking with them because we're too panicked or tense.

He went on to share some of the reasons why kids today are suffering more than previous generations. I loved his candor and his matter-of-fact way of communicating. He didn't pull his punches.

WHY MORE TEENS TODAY ARE SUFFERING FROM SEVERE ANXIETY

1. ELECTRONICS OFFER AN UNHEALTHY ESCAPE.

When he began with point number one, I immediately realized I should have already put my phone away in my pocket. *Oops.* We all know this. The constant access to digital devices lets kids (and us) escape uncomfortable emotions. Social media and games and texting friends helps kids avoid boredom, loneliness, and sadness. We're now seeing the consequences of an entire generation having spent their childhoods avoiding discomfort. Their electronics replaced opportunities to develop mental strength, and they didn't gain the coping skills they need to handle everyday challenges. This brought the instructor to his next point:

2. HAPPINESS IS ALL THE RAGE.

Bobby McFerrin's song "Don't Worry Be Happy" hit the airwaves in 1988. It was a huge hit, and the lyrics summed up America's mindset at the time, one characterized by the avoidance of all things emotionally difficult. The pursuit of happiness is emphasized so much in our culture that some parents think it's their job to make their kids happy, all of the time. The early 2000s brought us the helicopter parent: the mom or dad who hovers over their child's life, immersed in their academic pursuits and other day-to-day activities. When little Tommy feels sad, his parents feel the need to cheer him up. When little Tommy feels angry, they calm him down. Little Tommy has grown up believing that if he doesn't feel happy around the clock, then something must be wrong. And this has done more harm than good for Tommy. As he gets older it results in inner turmoil. Little Tommy never learned that it's normal and healthy to feel sad, frustrated, guilty, disappointed, and angry sometimes, too.

3. PARENTS ARE GIVING UNREALISTIC PRAISE.

When the instructor made this point, I immediately thought of my own life. My parents were super affirming. Like, to the point of delusion. I remember them telling me that I was the fastest kid in my school when I was in kindergarten. Kindergarten!! That's ridiculous! If I raced a fourth grader, I'd get killed. After my parents said this I remember feeling like I needed to hide the fact that I wasn't the fastest in school so I wouldn't let them down.

It's like the *Seinfeld* episode "The Race." As a kid, Jerry won a race. He'd gotten a head start, but no one really noticed except for his rival. To cover it up, Jerry never ran a race again for fear that his normal speed would be found out. Too funny!

We see this being played out in the extreme in the lives of kids today. Parents should affirm their kids—but they should be honest when they do. When parents say things like "You're the smartest kid in your grade," it doesn't actually build their self-esteem. Instead, it creates a mismatch between what the kid knows and what their parents are saying, which can lead to insecurity. Instead of affirming them, false praise puts pressure on kids to live up to those impossible statements. When they don't get that A+, well, it must be that stupid teacher's fault…or so some parents say. All of this can lead to kids' crippling fear of failure and rejection, or the inability to see themselves and their limitations clearly.

4. PARENTS ARE GETTING CAUGHT UP IN THE RAT RACE.

Many parents have become like personal assistants or Lyft drivers for their teenagers. Today's parents are working hard and doing everything they can to ensure their kids can compete at the highest level. So they hire tutors and private sports coaches and pay for expensive SAT courses. Many kids in our youth group have played on three or four soccer teams at the same time. Parents make it their job to help their children build resumés that will impress top schools. We all remember the actresses Felicity Huffman and Lori Loughlin, who ended up going to prison after paying crazy sums of money to falsify their daughters' resumés and ensure they got into the school of their choice. These are insane times! And this crazy pressure is not helping anyone's children at all. No duh, huh?

5. KIDS AREN'T LEARNING EMOTIONAL SKILLS.

In our anxiety class this point stood out. I see it in the youth I minister to. Our culture emphasizes academic preparation, but we put little effort into teaching our kids the emotional skills they need to succeed. In fact, a national survey of first-year college students revealed that 60% wished they had been more emotionally prepared for college life.[23] They are struggling, and the results are alarming. All of this reveals more about the adults in charge than the students. We aren't doing our jobs.

Think of what this feels like for teenagers. An eighteen-year-old heads off for their freshman year of college. They don't know how to manage their time or deal with their feelings. They're ill-prepared to handle and combat stress, so they pursue all things happy. The avoidance of discomfort comes at the expense of them learning necessary skills, which in turn does tremendous damage, further preventing them from leading good, meaningful, and healthy lives. Without vital coping skills, it's no wonder teens today are feeling anxious over everyday hassles. We've created an environment that fosters anxiety in young people rather than resilience. And while we can't prevent all anxiety disorders from occurring—there's definitely a genetic component, as well as sources of anxiety other than the ones we've looked at here—we can do a better job helping kids build the mental muscles they need to stay healthy.

6. A WORLD THAT FEELS SCARY AND THREATENING.

When I was living in Texas for a short time as a boy we regularly had tornado drills at school. Because of those darn drills, I feared tornados more than anything else. Today we've seen an increase in school shootings, with resulting drills and lockdowns in schools. We've seen coverage of shootings in public places. Shootings are discussed on the news nearly every week, if not every day. They're also bombarded with news of war. And then of course there are terrorist attacks around the world, which are also on the list of kids' fears.

Recently I was talking with an extreme conservative whom I love very much. He was sharing about his political views when his seven-year-old son interrupted us and said to me, "I hate when my dad talks about this. It scares me so much!" The father then said that he hates when his son says things like that. Well dude, your politics are scary! What and how we share conveys to our kids that the world is a scary place.

HOW TO RECOGNIZE ANXIETY IN TEENS

As I wrote earlier, nearly 32% of teenagers today have been diagnosed with an anxiety disorder. Many, many more have anxiety problems, but they haven't received help, or haven't been diagnosed. It's not always easy to tell when typical stress crosses over into anxiety in teenagers, but it is really important to know that problems with our mental health typically don't just go away—they tend to get worse rather than improving on their own. It's vital that we take it seriously when a kid comes to us with issues related to stress and anxiety.

Not long ago a mom called and asked if I could come over to the house. Her daughter wouldn't go to school. In fact, she wouldn't come out of her room, but she said she'd talk with me and Kelsey. We headed over. From the other side of the bedroom door I asked if it would be okay if Kelsey and I came in. Thankfully, the girl opened the door and immediately collapsed into our arms, crying. We learned that her anxiety disorder and her feelings of tension and fear had begun to interfere with her daily activities at home and school. In fact, the thought of going to school rendered her useless. She'd been seeing a counselor, but it wasn't the right fit. Her anxiety was too much for her to handle. It had begun to affect everything. We got her to a counselor friend of ours who was better equipped for her issues and personality and this began the journey toward healing.

Teens can be diagnosed with a number of different types of anxiety disorders, with a number of different symptoms. I want to cover a few that I've learned about in the years of dealing with these issues with our teens.

GENERALIZED ANXIETY DISORDER (GAD)

GAD is the most common teen anxiety disorder. In fact, one in three teenagers today will experience some form of anxiety disorder, and more than likely it will be GAD.[24] Children as young as six years of age can begin to show symptoms. In teenagers, this type of anxiety involves obsessive worry over everyday events that lasts for a prolonged period of time. If you have a teen who is experiencing intense emotional stress as well as a range of anxiety-related symptoms, they likely have GAD. Teens with GAD not only experience excessive worrying but also extreme low self-esteem.[25]

GAD symptoms include:

- Inability to control feelings of worry and stress
- Restlessness or edginess
- Fatigue
- Irritability
- Muscle tension
- Sleep problems

After the anxiety class, I talked more with the instructor. He said that researchers believe that general anxiety disorders involve a disruption in how the brain reacts to the signals it uses to identify and confront danger. Sometimes this looks like a kid with GAD overreacting to something that seems normal. Fortunately, GAD is very treatable.

SOCIAL ANXIETY DISORDER

Social anxiety affects over forty million people living in the United States. The typical age of onset is around thirteen years old.[26] Social anxiety disorder—also referred to as social phobia—is when a person is overcome with fear and worry in social settings. For teenagers, this type of anxiety negatively impacts daily life. Typically, a person with a social phobia experiences intense anxiety that leads to deep feelings of embarrassment and fear of being judged by others. Consequently, a teen with social phobia often withdraws and avoids contact with peers or adults. Social anxiety can be paralyzing for teenagers at youth group, in school, and at family gatherings.

Additional social anxiety symptoms include:

- Feeling nauseous
- Sweating
- Nervous shaking

- Unexpected blushing
- Fear of having to talk or perform in front of a group

ANXIETY ATTACKS

I received a phone call one evening. "Brock, can I come over, like, right now?"

It was one of our high school seniors. "Of course, come on over," I replied. After he arrived he began to tell me that he'd been having anxiety attacks every day for the past three weeks. He said he just couldn't do it anymore.

We talked about his life, his thinking, his relationships, and his schedule. What I discovered was that his schedule was insane: late nights, early mornings, massive pressure, and no end in sight. I asked if there was anything he could cut from his schedule. He said no, that there was nothing he could get around or out of. I felt like the situation was above my pay grade, so I took him the next day to a counselor who was a volunteer on our youth ministry team.

Unlike panic attacks, anxiety attacks are reactions to external stressors. An anxiety attack is typically a symptom of an anxiety disorder. Not everyone with an anxiety disorder will experience anxiety attacks. Anxiety attacks result when an individual encounters a specific stressor.[27]

A person undergoing an anxiety attack will often experience any or all of the following symptoms:

- Feeling fearful or full of dread
- Shortness of breath
- Racing heart
- Cold sweats
- Dizziness and wooziness

Anxiety attacks tend to be short-lived, passing once the stressor is removed.

Symptoms of anxiety attacks tend to be less extreme than the physical symptoms of panic attacks.

PANIC DISORDER

Panic disorder is quite common. Approximately six million adults in the United States experience panic disorders.[28] Panic disorders can begin in childhood or early adolescence, although they tend to set in during late adolescence or early adulthood. Girls are twice as likely as boys to suffer from panic disorders. A panic disorder involves a fear of disaster or of losing control, even when there is no apparent danger. Thus, people with panic disorder have a sudden and often unexpected period of intense fear. Many people believe they are having a heart attack the first time they have a panic attack.

Panic attacks are the main symptom of a panic disorder. Sometimes panic attacks are triggered by the thought of an anxiety-producing event that's coming up in the future, or even by the fear of having another panic attack.

The symptoms of panic disorder may include the following:

- Rapid chest palpitations
- Accelerated heart rate
- Sweating
- Shaking
- Nausea
- Chills
- Dizziness
- Breathing problems

It's important to note that panic disorders often run in families. A teen with a family history of panic disorders is more susceptible.

In later chapters we'll get into how to respond and lead our students more holistically. First it's important to get an understanding of the symptoms of anxiety disorders and how they play out. This is the world they are waking up to every morning.

THE ANXIOUS TEEN

Week after week Ashton and I sat next to each other in that anxiety class and I watched him and others slowly get stronger, find hope, and develop skills for the way forward. Still, I felt that as youth workers we were just scratching the surface.

This whole topic can be overwhelming. To be honest, I remember being extremely hesitant to even write this book. But it was a topic I couldn't stop thinking about. When I was considering writing another book I drove down to San Diego to talk with Marko, the head of The Youth Cartel, and I pitched him about five different book ideas I'd been mulling over for the past year or two. I saved the idea of teen anxiety for last because honestly, it felt too overwhelming to spend a couple of years writing and editing about this topic. But Marko was convinced. "Brock, you have to write this book!" he said. "This is the world our youth workers must learn to navigate." Our prayer is that you as youth workers will learn from these pages and that this book will help you gain strategies to use in your ministry.

CHAPTER TAKEAWAYS

- It's not always obvious from the outside which of our students is struggling with anxiety or other aspects of mental health.

- More teens today are suffering from severe anxiety than in the past, for a host of reasons.

- Learning more about different types of anxiety and related issues (like generalized anxiety disorder, social anxiety disorder, anxiety attacks, and panic disorder) can help us walk alongside and support our teenagers.

NOTES *from a Mental Health Therapist*

I love that Brock offered a class on stress and anxiety relief. I also love that he had a great turnout—although I do wish these classes weren't so needed.

The "pursuit of happiness culture" discussed in this chapter often begins in the homes that pull for "well-behaved" kids. These are the homes that relegate "bad attitudes" to your room until you can behave better. The unspoken message is that we should manage our negative feelings alone, and when we are happy again we may participate with others. In the church community, the pursuit of the happiness culture creates an environment where anything unpleasant or difficult is swept under the rug. Teens are often left believing that their anxieties don't have a place in the home or the church.

The challenge is that teens are great at hiding anxiety. Adults wanting to help sometimes have to see beyond what the teen is saying and look to their behavior. I often tell people in my sessions that mind-reading is never a good idea. I want to clarify, though, that reading behavior is not mind-reading (and please don't try to read the teen's mind).

If a teen isn't willing or able to see their anxiety and address it, then the anxiety will be played out—it's just a question of how. Some teens exhibit external behaviors, while others turn inward. External behaviors include things like getting into fights or bullying others. Internal behaviors include self-harm.

One common piece of advice is, "if you see a teen's behavior change, then something is going on." For instance, if a once outspoken teen becomes quiet, chances are that something has shifted for them and they are struggling. That is psychology 101. Sometimes, though, anxiety in our kids is hiding in plain sight in behaviors that are true to form. For example, teens being on their phones. What is sometimes the normal behavior of a healthy teen can also a be way that the teen is managing their anxiety. The actual act of swiping could be a technique to maintain calm...at least temporarily. (When we avoid anxiety instead of addressing it or acknowledging it, anxiety grows.) Holding a phone can be physically soothing, a more advanced version of a fidget spinner. There can also be anxiety underlying choices in school, like in teens who sit in the same spot week after week. They might do this because it feels "right" and it's their comfort zone. But being in the comfort zone could be a means of avoiding anxiety.

All teens will experience anxiety as some point. It's important to hold onto this truth. We don't need to pathologize all anxiety, or create a message that something is wrong with me if I do feel anxious. The goal of helping teens with their anxiety is not to do away with all anxiety; that goes back to the happiness culture. The goal is to help teens recognize whether the stress and anxiety they are experiencing is normal, or something bigger, and then help them move through   not run away from—the discomfort of those difficult feelings.

Groovy Brains

I'm sitting in a coffee shop in Lincoln City, Oregon, looking out at the vast ocean. It's an incredible sight. The Pacific looks so cold and dark, ominous and powerful. As a below-average surfer, even *thinking* about getting in sounds insane. Just by looking I can tell that below the surface, the current is forceful. It kind of takes my breath away.

Many psychologists refer to the mental world as being like a sea. It's deep and vast, full of great hopes and dreams, overwhelming feelings, magnificent thoughts. It can be warm and inviting, teeming with tender feelings and thoughts of love. It's also a place of immense turmoil. The turbulence of regret and sorrow overwhelms us along with the nightmarish dread of haunting fears, often seeming to lurk at unknown depths.

In the past most scientific experts believed that what happened in the life of babies and small children didn't really have much impact on them later in life. They could be surrounded by turmoil and chaos as infants, but wouldn't really remember all of the trauma. It was a gift of being young. But now what we're hearing is just the opposite. We are learning that the body and the brain remember.

My mom has an amazing ministry to single moms up in the Northwest. She walks alongside them, these many mothers who have absolutely been through it. Their stories are difficult to hear. But there they are, trying to overcome the obstacles while raising children all by themselves. And their kids, almost across the board, start to implode between the ages of eight and twelve. All of a sudden they begin to have fits of rage or become plagued with overwhelming social anxiety or experience crippling fears and eventually addictive behaviors. Many of these mothers' children go to school, where they work all day to keep it together emotionally—but when they come home in the evening, they fall apart. It takes everything within them not to act out at school and they run out of steam by day's end. Many of them have been diagnosed with ADHD or even PTSD.

The odd thing is that a lot of these kids were babies when their parents divorced or split up and when other traumas occurred. The most chaotic points of their lives came when they were very, very young. They've often been raised for a number of years in a fairly stable home. But again, the body remembers.

A child's developing brain is most flexible during the earliest months and years of life. During this time period, the foundation is set for lifelong health and well-being…or the opposite. We now know that the early part of a person's life is the most important. Ninety percent of brain growth happens before kindergarten.[29] The environment a child is raised in dramatically impacts the formation of the brain. If a parent is having anxiety issues or there is tension in the home for any reason, it impacts the child's developing brain.

In his book *Mindsight*, Dr. Dan Siegel writes about how mirror neurons in the brain help soak in information and enable us to learn.[30] You've heard that children's brains are like sponges, absorbing everything around them? Well, this is true, and it's because of these mirror neurons. As Siegel writes, "They are the antennae in the brain that pick up information about the intentions and feelings of others, and they create in us both emotional resonance and behavioral imitation."[31] Basically, a child's brain will mirror the internal state of the people around them, simply by observing their behavior. And this mirroring literally shapes the brain, building bridges and unique grooves within it, pathways that affect their responses to future triggers. For any child growing up in an anxious and fearful world (that's all of them), what they're experiencing is impacting their brain development.

In his book *The Body Keeps The Score*, Dr. Bessel van der Kolk writes about how early maltreatment of a child has lasting and enduring negative effects on brain development. Our brains are sculpted by our early experiences.

That word, *sculpted*, is key. Any kind of difficulty or mistreatment, any kind of abuse or neglect, or even a stressful environment, is like a chisel that shapes a brain to contend with strife, but at the cost of deep, enduring wounds.[32]

The brain is literally shaped by the experiences of our early years. They sculpt and etch into childhood brains.

Early childhood trauma is widespread and comes in many forms. So if you have kids with divorced parents in your youth group, or adopted kids, or kids whose parents who are struggling with their own fears and anxieties, or kids who've been neglected or have been raised around drug abuse or alcoholism, or kids with parents who deal with anger or depression, or kids whose parents are workaholics and are never around, or kids whose parents have addictions, or kids whose parents went through a season of unemployment and it created an imbalance in the home…then what you have are kids whose brains have been sculpted and shaped by those experiences. Their brains have been mirroring what they've seen in those around them. Within these kids' brains, all of this has developed patterns and grooves that cause some impairment to normal functioning.

As youth workers, many times we are unaware of what may be going on in the brains of our youth. We don't always look at a teenager and realize there are patterns in their brain that make it extremely difficult for them to cope with everyday ups and downs, let alone deal with bigger struggles. So they come to our youth groups and we play some games and give them a little Jesus and then they jump into small groups and barely scratch the surface of what is going on inside of them. This just isn't cutting it for a generation of kids plagued by anxiety, addictions, anger, apathy, or any other "a" word that you can think of.

What we're typically doing just isn't enough. It isn't thoughtful enough. It isn't deep enough. It isn't spiritual enough. How can we do better?

What if more and more youth ministries were places of sanctuary and healing and wholeness and vision, rather than places that provided safe and entertaining religion?

THE ANXIOUS TEEN

Many youth workers and teachers and counselors are tackling these issues head-on, and they're doing their best to partner together to bring restorative and healing work to the lives of today's kids.

Kids like Matthew. When I became his youth pastor he was happy to meet me. He was friendly and open to a relationship, but he had deep and profound insecurities and, we'd later discover, a violent temper. If he ever felt left out or marginalized or ignored he'd act out. Any time he felt unheard or misunderstood, he became violently angry.

I found out that Matthew had spent the first three years of his life in an orphanage in Russia before he was adopted. His adoptive parents brought this neglected and forgotten toddler to their home in the U.S. Matthew had no conscious memory of his years in the orphanage, but his body sure did remember. And anytime something would happen that reminded his brain about his years of neglect and abuse, his body would go into survival mode. This is what led him to respond physically to disappointment and conflict.

Or take Stephanie. She was raised in the Northeast by successful, wealthy parents, but her mom and dad struggled in their marriage and their home was filled with chaos and stress. From the outside her life seemed ideal, but by the time Stephanie was in tenth grade she began to confide in us about the difficulties at home. Hearing her parents fighting in the car since she was a baby had shaped her. As a result, she developed an amazing ability to avoid and escape anything that made her feel uncomfortable. But now the stress of school was something she could not avoid, and so she fell into horrendous habits to numb all of the pain.

Then there is Mary. Her parents got divorced when she was little. When Mary decided to live with her mom, her dad decided he was done with her. She wouldn't hear from him for months at a time. When she'd text him or leave him a message, he wouldn't respond. I met her when she was skateboarding in our church parking lot when she was eleven years old. We invited her to youth group and she jumped right in. Mary came across as happy and super relational. What we didn't know was that the boys in the neighborhood knew she was an easy target to take advantage of sexually. They began to pass her around like a cheap bottle of whiskey. Her father's rejection had negatively shaped her view of herself. This deeply grooved pathway in her brain led to more damage and trauma.

I think of Caleb. We first met at my first-ever youth group when I was the new youth pastor. He immediately began to talk my ear off. Like seriously, nonstop chatter. That first day I could hardly meet anyone else because Caleb was dominating my time. As with all of these other students, once I learned his story I could understand what had shaped him. Caleb was a kid raised in a home where he was never listened to. Never taken seriously. He was neglected and he learned that if he didn't keep someone's attention, if he took a breath and didn't keep talking, then he'd lose them and never get 'em back. This became a self-fulfilling prophecy. Kids were annoyed by him, leaders were careful to avoid him, and there he was, with this gaping hole in his heart, aching just to be seen, to be heard.

About fifteen years ago I began noticing that there were issues with students that I, as a professional youth worker, was just not equipped to deal with. I knew that I needed to begin a partnership with other professionals in my city to work together in helping students who were struggling. I started to teach students coping skills and different forms of meditation, which I'll share more about later, but I quickly realized it would take a village of adults with differing expertise to help today's kids.

We needed a fellowship of adults to surround every kid. I needed to get some folks who understood these groovy-brained kids and how to heal and restore the damage. There were just too many patterns and learned behaviors that I couldn't fix alone, even with passionate prayer and relational ministry. The Lone Ranger "do it all myself" mentality had to die in me. I knew I needed help in getting them help.

When my daughter was in second grade she was diagnosed with a learning disability. This was one of my greatest fears because of my own story with a learning issue. Before her diagnosis, we weren't sure what was going on. Around that time I was speaking during the main service at our church when I mentioned something about my daughter and her struggle, a struggle at that time we didn't yet understand. I don't remember exactly what I said, but someone in our church was an occupational therapist who recognized the issue based on my words. She contacted our family and offered to diagnose and treat our daughter. This occupational therapist had recently learned of an experimental treatment she thought might be helpful in our case and wanted to try it out, using our daughter as a guinea pig. We immediately started appointments with her, and for the next year my daughter went to this amazingly gifted therapist who worked on rewiring Dancin's brain. Through light, rhythms, and balance exercises, our daughter slowly began to get better. We were amazed, and it honestly changed our girl's life.

I've also learned from the story of an amazing woman whom I love very much, my aunt. As a little girl she experienced great pain and suffering. Her story is dramatic and filled with incredible trauma. As an adult, she read about how childhood trauma causes grooves in the brain and how there was new psychotherapy to address it called Eye Movement Desensitization and Reprocessing (EMDR). EMDR is a fairly new and nontraditional type of psychotherapy that's growing in popularity, particularly for treating post-traumatic stress disorder. She was desperate, so she went for some sessions.

It took a while, but through these sessions she began to experience healing for the first time. My aunt's groovy brain was slowly becoming rewired.[33]

What I hope all of these examples show is that we must minister with an awareness that there's a lot going on below the surface of anyone's life. We must treat and minister to the whole person. Any given youth worker will quickly find themselves out of their depth, so we've gotta get out from behind the walls of our churches and partner with experts in our communities.

Can you imagine being on a caring, educated, and proactive team of parents, coaches, therapists, and spiritual directors? How amazing would it be to have a youth ministry approach that brings all of these people together to rescue a generation that is struggling? This is the dream, a dream that will launch kids into adulthood having experienced some healing and having learned some skills that will help them navigate the road ahead.

The ocean can be dark and turbulent, and sometimes our kids feel like they're drowning. If we recognize what is happening and partner together to help bring healing and wholeness, we can also bring hope to this generation.

CHAPTER TAKEAWAYS

- What happens during the earliest years of a person's life has a profound impact—even if they're too young to consciously remember it later. The brain is shaped by the experiences of our early years.

- Youth ministries should work to become places of sanctuary and healing and wholeness and vision, rather than places for safe and entertaining religion.

- We need a team of adults to surround, support, and love every kid, especially those impacted by trauma and mental health illnesses.

NOTES *from a Mental Health Therapist*

Part of the process of becoming a licensed therapist is what's known as the associateship. In my day, it was called an internship. After you graduate with a master's degree, this is the period that comes prior to the licensing test. During the associateship you see clients and are supervised by a licensed therapist. Associates are typically eager to prove to the world (and by "the world" I mean their supervisors and themselves) that they know what they are doing. During the associateship, you say yes to working with all types of clients. It's a time for discerning what clientele you work best with, for noticing where you find your footing and where you struggle. It is a time of finding a place to work out of that's somewhere between the fear of "how do I do this?" and the overconfidence of "I can fix them all."

It was during my associateship when I learned about my limitations. A client was referred to me, someone I hadn't talked to prior to our meeting in my office. He came in on a late afternoon. As I listened to this man's story and heard what he was hoping for from therapy, I was filled with angst. In my head was everything I'd learned in school. I heard my supervisor's voice going over the interventions to use. I knew what I could do in our session. The problem was that all of this knowledge wasn't enough. I had a pit in my stomach.

THE ANXIOUS TEEN

It was only in discussing what I'd experienced with my own therapist the next day that I realized I'd encountered my own limits. I was feeling fear. I had heard this man's story and I knew the next steps to help him with healing—but I also knew something else: I was not the person best suited to be his therapist. I needed to refer him to someone better equipped.

This was important knowledge. This story came back to my mind when I read what Brock shared about Matthew. Brock knew his limits, and knew he needed a team to support Matthew. It's important to recognize our limits, and to know when it's time to reach out to others.

We also need to maintain healthy boundaries. Boundaries help to define where I end and the other person starts. They are vital when working with someone who is struggling. We don't need to take on their struggle to help them.

We need to have a trusted team around us. Those people can connect and help others when we're not the right fit, and they can also be our sounding board when we need support. We also need to pay attention to our own feelings as we spend time with people who are struggling, asking discerning questions: *Is this angst I am feeling about me? Or is it God whispering that I need to step aside and involve another person or a bigger team? Is it time for me to become part of, rather than all of, what is necessary for this person's healing?*

Suicide

From 2015 to 2022 I went to teen residential mental hospitals nearly fifty times to visit students I was ministering to. If you've ever been to one, you won't forget it. Kids walking around in slippers and hospital nightgowns with their dyed hair and adolescent angst. What's least forgettable is the feeling of places like this. There's a haunting sickness in the air and a myriad of emotions: pain, dysfunction, brokenness, fear, and a touch of hope. Just a touch, though.

You cannot label the "type" of kid who will struggle with mental health. No socioeconomic level or life experience is immune. The only defining and common characteristics are that all of these teens have easy access to smartphones and technology, and have grown up in a world that's been shaped by them.

I remember receiving a phone call from a father who had found some of his son's artwork and poetry. What this dad found was so dark and hopeless, so focused on death, that it scared him. He talked to his son, who had finally admitted that he didn't want to live anymore. That life was too hard and there wasn't any sign that it could get better. This scared the father even more. He asked me over the phone what he should do. I said, "Take him right now to the emergency room."

I've learned that in cases like these, it is way better to overreact than to under-react. To under-react could lead to something unthinkable. So I was clear in what I told this man. "Take him to the hospital emergency room and tell them what's going on. They will assess the situation and get you to the right place."

My approach, when these kinds of serious concerns arise, is to get kids in quickly and, as soon as you can, get them out of there. Those places are super helpful in cases of an emergency, but they are also pretty dark. Get them in for the help they need, and get them out for the life they're going to lead. (And yes, I'm a poet and I didn't even know it.)

Within hours this young man was placed in a teen psychiatric hospital and began to get the kind of help he needed.

I headed over to the hospital a day after he was checked in. I can only describe how he looked as *lighter*. Something had changed in him since the last time I'd seen him. We sat in his room together and he told me how he was feeling. "I just got into this rut of negativity and darkness and hopelessness. For the first time in years I feel like I'm going to be okay." I was relieved and told him how proud I was of him.

Several years ago I received another phone call, this time from the mother of one of the girls in our youth group. This girl had spent time in and out of teen psychiatric hospitals. Her mom said things were bad with her daughter's mental health. As the story goes, she and her daughter were shopping at a mall when the daughter went to use the restroom. A couple of minutes later someone came running out of the bathroom asking for help—a girl in the bathroom was trying to hang herself. Not long after that terrible and unthinkable scene, this girl became another of the kids I visited in a residential facility.

At youth group one night, a fourteen-year-old girl asked me if we could talk. She and her family have a great relationship with me and my wife, and with our middle school pastor, Bekah. The girl told me what had happened: "I did it again. I had sex this week with three different guys and I feel completely out of control. I can't stop myself!" I asked her if we could talk with Bekah and we set up a time for the three of us to meet. Before we could get together, I received a phone call that an explosive fight had happened at this girl's home, and afterward she'd attempted suicide with pills.

The mother asked me if I could get over to the hospital to meet with her daughter as soon as possible. While I was on my way there, this girl escaped. As I drove up to the hospital, I saw her running down the street, barefoot and in a hospital gown. I couldn't believe my eyes. I sped over to her, opened the passenger car door, and she jumped into my car. I parked and we walked back into the hospital together.

These are things a youth worker never forgets. Not only was she suicidal at fourteen, but she already had a sex addiction. Youth ministry these days, huh?

Suicide is now the second leading cause of death in young people ages fifteen to twenty-four, just behind car accidents. As the CDC reports:

Boys are four times more likely to die from suicide than girls.
Girls are more likely to try to commit suicide than boys.
Guns are used in more than half of all youth suicides.[34]

According to the CDC, the numbers have climbed dramatically since the pandemic began.[35] I'm sure the reported statistics will indicate this in the coming years. The trends are not good. As stated in U.S. News and World Report,

Emergency room visits for suspected suicide attempts among girls between the ages of 12 and 17 increased by 26% during summer 2020 and by 50% during winter 2021, compared with the same periods in 2019, researchers from the U.S. Centers for Disease Control and Prevention found.[36]

The same study indicated that "young girls might have been more affected by the pandemic due to lockdowns that broke their connectedness to schools, teachers and friends..."[37] This is concerning. We also have to recognize that these numbers have been on the rise since 2010. This is not something we can solely chalk up to the pandemic. According to the CDC, "the rate of suicide for those ages 10 to 24 increased nearly 60% between 2007 and 2018..."[38]

THE ANXIOUS TEEN

There are many psychological, environmental, and social reasons why a teen would feel the need to end their life. According to the National Institute of Mental Health, most kids who attempt suicide are in the midst of depression and often have a combination of other mental disorders. Then you throw in some other factors like disciplinary problems, interpersonal losses, family violence, sexual orientation confusion, physical and sexual abuse, and being the victim of bullying. These are lethal combinations that we must be aware of.[39]

While suicide is on the rise, it is still a rare event. Nevertheless, we as youth workers must be ready when it happens. And we, along with our small group leaders, must be aware of the common signs in the lives of these precious ones. Here are some of them:

- Talking about dying: Any mention of dying, disappearing, jumping, shooting oneself, or other type of self-harm.

- Recent loss: Through death, divorce, separation, broken relationship, self-confidence, self-esteem, loss of interest in friends, hobbies, or activities previously enjoyed.

- Change in personality: Sad, withdrawn, irritable, anxious, tired, indecisive, apathetic.

- Change in behavior: Can't concentrate on school, work, or routine tasks.

- Change in sleep patterns: Insomnia, often with early waking or oversleeping, or nightmares.

- Change in eating habits: Loss of appetite and weight, or overeating.

- Fear of losing control: Acting erratically, harming self or others.

- Low self-esteem: Feeling worthless, shame, overwhelming guilt, self-hatred, "everyone would be better off without me."

- No hope for the future: Believing things will never get better, or that nothing will ever change.[40]

As I'm writing this, it is finals week all over the country. This past Wednesday I heard from our small group leaders that kids' stress and anxiety levels seemed higher than they had been in a long time. When I got home from youth group the other day, I opened my Instagram and saw that the U.S. Surgeon General had actually issued an advisory warning about young people's mental health. He said that we all need to be looking for signs of mental anxiety and depression among teenagers.

One in four of the kids who go to your youth group and attend the schools in your community have contemplated or are contemplating their suicide. That's the reality of what the suicide statistics mean for our lives.

But here's an important truth in the midst of this: People make all the difference. Research tells us that if people notice the signs, and get the vulnerable person to a psychiatric hospital, lives are saved.[41] Small group leaders, youth pastors, parents, coaches, teachers, and counselors all need to be on high alert. It's better to overreact, get the teenager to a facility where they can receive help, and be wrong about them needing it than it is to underreact and end up at a funeral. I cringe as I write that, but it's true.

I love the helpful dos and don'ts Dr. Lilia Mucka Andrew and Dr. Erin M. Sadler offer on how to talk to kids about suicide. It applies for parents and for youth workers—anyone who works with young people. I've included some of their advice in the excerpt below:

DO stay calm.

DO be direct. Ask them, "Are you thinking of suicide?"

DO reassure. Let your child know that there is help and that this feeling will not last forever. Ask your child what you can do for them during moments of distress, whether it is sitting with them, giving them a hug or doing a shared activity together.

DO remove means for self-harm.

DO NOT judge. Be a safe place for them in their distress. Reflect the pain they are experiencing and show empathy and validation.

DO NOT leave them alone.[42]

THE ANXIOUS TEEN

Andrew and Sadler go on to write that sometimes you may feel uncertain of whether a teen is safe, or you may be unsure how to talk with them. If this occurs, call 911 or take them to the emergency department for a safety assessment. You can also contact the National Suicide Prevention Lifeline for help: 988.[43]

A REASON TO HOPE

Recently, someone asked me why I haven't gone and planted a church. Why wasn't I a lead pastor somewhere? I smirked as I said, "Because I like being where the action is." Honestly, though, I don't want to miss out on what I sense is coming. Our culture is moving toward an important moment. All of the pressure and tension and pain and desperation I've been writing about in these pages is leading to something, and I believe that "something" is hope. As youth workers, we get to be hope dealers. Everywhere we go, we get to be bearers of this really amazing, over-the-top, awesome news. And we get to bring it to a generation that has ears to hear. Why? Because nothing else is working for them.

Last night we were driving together around our city as a family. My wife and I were singing to some Foo Fighters up front when our daughter interrupted. "Can you pray for me right now please? I'm feeling really overwhelmed and full of anxiety." She told us that she was really stressed about a meeting she had scheduled with her boss for the next day. We prayed together, and she began to sense the peace of God break into her heart and mind.

After that I talked to her about an idea related to what she was going through. It's something that can seem a little weird, like a backward concept: It's the fact that we are residents of the future.

Let me explain.

Followers of Jesus can actually live on the other side of difficulty. It's why the early followers of Jesus could go through incredible suffering and maintain hope. They knew that on the other side of anything difficult, painful, stressful, or scary, there was good to come. We can apply this to ourselves. We know what's coming. We are residents of the future. When we take in the words and teachings of Jesus, we know that on the other side of that meeting—or any stressful, anxiety-producing thing—is good. God is walking into that meeting and he is with us. He is with us in every hard conversation and in everything that happens afterward. Even when things don't go well, he is with us. This isn't a trite sentiment. It's why we can live with hope in difficult moments, difficult weeks, and even in difficult seasons. We'll look at this more in the chapter called "Future Hope." But as we talked, Kelsey and I watched peace grow in our lovely daughter. We saw strength come to her. Even her posture changed.

The morning light breaks in when caring adults are on the lookout for kids who are hurting and struggling. We are hope dealers.

- Hope asks questions.
- Hope listens.
- Hope speaks vision.
- Hope reminds them who they are.
- Hope gets them help, because their future is a blessed one.
- Hope drives them to a counselor and waits outside to take them home afterward.
- Hope prays with desperate parents.
- Hope creates an environment of vulnerability, where kids feel safe to be their weakest selves.

Why? Because in our weakness, God is stronger. We don't have to pretend anymore. Once we admit our struggles, our faults, our brokenness, then we can move forward. There is power in sharing weakness. The morning light can break into the dark moment.

You've heard it said that it's always darkest before dawn. Whether or not that is literally true, I certainly do love the notion. What is true for sure is that it is often coldest before dawn. Just before the sun comes up, it can be bleak. But that bleakness, that darkness, that chilly temperature means we are closest to where the light will break in. I just love that idea. Morning is coming. The dawn is about to break.

THE ANXIOUS TEEN

CHAPTER TAKEAWAYS

- There is no one "type" of kid who will struggle with mental health. Mental health issues span all races, genders, abilities, and socioeconomic statuses.

- All youth workers and volunteers need to be aware of the signs of suicidal tendencies.

- When someone shows suicidal tendencies, take them seriously right away and respond by seeking appropriate, professional treatment.

- Asking someone if they are suicidal will not plant the idea in their head.

NOTES *from a Mental Health Therapist*

Isn't "suicide" a scary word? Just this last week I have heard two stories that people who "we would never have guessed" died by suicide. These stories are happening too often, and are always tragic.

I am so glad that Brock has a chapter dedicated to this topic. I want to add my own two cents, from the therapist's side of things.

It is super important to distinguish between self-harm and suicidal tendencies. Parents will call terrified that their teen is suicidal based on seeing signs of self-harm. It is important to note that self-harm is not suicidal behavior. That's true even if (although I know this sounds scary) the wound they created is deep enough to require stitches. Teens who self-harm are not always suicidal. Cutting with a sharp object is the form of self-harm I have encountered most, although teens often burn themselves as well. I have known teens who cut with objects like paper clips or the end of a pencil with the eraser removed. (One note: self-harm is not excessive piercings or tattoos.)

Self-harm is actually a coping skill. It is a way for teens to manage their anxieties and depression. Teens will tell you that it is better to experience physical pain rather than emotional pain, and that the act of harming acts as a release.

When we learn a teen is self-harming, we need to avoid inducing shame. The best question is, "How can I help?" versus, "Why would you do that?"

Having said that, self-harm always calls for a mental health evaluation. Please don't believe your teen when they tell you, "I'm okay, it was a one-time thing." Please seek help.

For those of you who are youth workers, please don't keep this information from the teen's parent. I have heard many times that youth leaders didn't get parents involved in instances of self-harm or suicidal thoughts because the teen convinced them not to.

If you suspect a teen is suicidal, please ask them about it. Be direct. Asking a teen if they are suicidal will *not* put the thought into their head. Teens will be honest with you. They will tell you if they are suicidal, or have ever thought about suicide. If they are thinking about suicide, seek help. If they have thought about suicide in the past although they aren't now, seek help.

I have been part of a few conversations with parents where it is decided that their suicidal teen will "work with" their youth leader. This is never the right approach. Youth leaders and counselors have different skill sets. Counselors are trained for this. Allow them to help you.

Teens don't often appreciate when parents or other adults become eagle-eyed after learning of self-harm or suicidal behavior. It is important to keep your eyes open and to maintain a constant presence around them, but hovering creates issues for the teen. Despite the intention of adults to be caring and aware, teens can, and will, become more secretive if they are being watched too closely.

Parents are too often surprised at where teens can hide things. They think they know what it is like for their kids because "I was a teen once." This isn't exactly true: Adults were never teens in this day and age.

It is also important to recognize that teens are more than just their self-harm or suicidal ideation or behavior. Don't let the fear of what could happen cloud your whole view of the person in front of you. This is the same person you knew prior to hearing that they were self-harming or suicidal. These new truths don't change that. Teens are very aware of when adults ask them questions that are shrouded in care, but are really just wanting to know whether they are "better" or still suicidal. Continue to be the person you are to them. Continue the relationship you had with them prior to this new knowledge.

Pressure

I work at a great church in Southern California called The Bridge. The best thing about our church is the kids' ministry pastor. Her name is Kelsey and she is super talented: bright, thoughtful, a gifted communicator with a huge heart. She also just so happens to be my wife.

Every Wednesday night after church Kelsey and I download together all that happened during our evening programs. Often we share sweet God moments: A fifth grade boy leading his small group prayer time, how into worship kids were, the great question a teenager asked, moments of real depth. We also go over other kinds of moments, the moments that make you want to laugh, or cry, or laugh and cry at the same time.

Last night I told her about an eighth grade girl who has been isolating herself more and more. She's become the kid in black with the sweatshirt hood pulled over her head, sitting in the back corner. Most people get the hint and just leave her alone. But not me. Every week I go and sit with her and we talk. Or I should say, I talk. Man, I am longing to see a breakthrough happen in her life. I am longing to see the heaviness lifted. I've seen it happen so many other times in kids like her. I know her story and it's not an easy one. The amount of pressure she has felt to be the perfect daughter, the perfect student, the perfect athlete was just too much for her. She feels like she's never lived up to anyone's expectations, so it makes sense that she's rebelling. But really, as she pulls back from other people she is asking, "Will you love me even if I give you nothing?"

THE ANXIOUS TEEN

Kelsey told me about a fourth grade boy who had to be asked to stop throwing balls and hitting the girls in their faces. Sounds like fun to me, but I guess the girls weren't really liking it for some reason. When he was warmly confronted, he responded by freaking out. He ran screaming into the corner and began hyperventilating. Kelsey had to use some counting techniques to help him with his breathing. After he calmed down a bit she sat with him and listened to more of his story. He talked about the overwhelming pressure he feels at home and at school. As the walls came down he admitted, "I don't think anyone likes me." Well, stop hitting people in the face with balls, dude. It's such a balance between grace and truth, isn't it?

Here's the thing: If you're a youth worker, these stories are super familiar. What I shared is just part of what happened on one single night! This is a fraction of what happens on any given day.

The following statistics from the Pew Research Center give us a picture of what teens are experiencing. Seventy percent of teenagers say that anxiety and depression are a major problem in their lives. Fifty-five percent say they have experienced bullying firsthand. These are huge numbers! When it comes to the sources of pressure teens face, academics tops the list, with 61% saying they feel a lot of pressure to get good grades. Throw in the fact that around 30% say they feel constant pressure to look good and to fit in socially and it's no wonder things are at a boiling point.[44]

Two years ago, my family moved back to Southern California right in the middle of the pandemic. We had been back East for the last ten years, so we were excited to get back to family and friends on the Best Coast. Sorry, East Coast people.

There's a vibe out here that's laid back, chill, and like, *Whatever man*. It's a mentality I really like—but it's also mostly a farce. Yes, people are warm like the weather, but below the surface the struggle is just as real. I was talking with about ten teenagers in our youth group about anxiety. Across the board they were like, "Nah, we're good. We don't have any anxiety." One of the keys to conversation with teenagers about anxiety and depression is knowing not to stop with the first question. What matters more are the follow-up questions. We have to be curious and keep scratching and digging to learn more in a way that doesn't scare them off. As youth workers, we've got to keep going after it. With these particular kids, I didn't let the topic drop. I kept talking. I started directing the questions away from them personally and toward their friends and *their* anxiety. This worked. While they hadn't shared about their own feelings with any real transparency, they were completely fine to admit that their friends were struggling.

And then it happened: A girl looked at the group and said, "I think we all feel the pressure around us." Boom, there it was—a way into a deeper conversation. They didn't like the word *anxious*, but *pressure* worked. Maybe it felt more California. Her statement opened a wonderful can of worms and by the end of our conversation the students were all sharing about school pressure, social media pressure, pressure their parents put on them, peer pressure, pressure to be awesome at everything, and the pressure they feel about what to do after high school. On and on they went.

My response was to validate what they were saying. So many adults tend to dismiss what teenagers say or even try to one-up them. A teenage girl recently told me that she told her mom she was struggling with her body image. Her mom's reaction? "You think you're dealing with body image? Trying being forty, kid!"

We can't one-up them. What they're experiencing is real. At this gathering I just hung in there, listening and affirming what they shared. Later I set up some meetings between them and me or their small group leader, making sure to do this especially for the students who really needed that follow-up. Kids who are in healthy, authentic friendships with caring adults can make progress in overcoming these emotional challenges.

The pressure kids are feeling from their peers has never been greater. Peer pressure was a thing we started to hear more about in the 1980s. I remember a 1987 commercial that a young Drew Barrymore was in. It was a "just say no" commercial with the first lady, Nancy Reagan. Of course we'd see in later interviews that despite the image she was projecting at that time, Drew was in deep trouble with drugs. The pressure was just too much, especially considering her home life. Fast forward to today, when kids are feeling all kinds of pressure that those of us born before the early 2000s can't comprehend. There is nothing similar in our frame of reference.

A couple of years ago a girl in our youth group asked if she could meet with me. She was an incredible basketball player and an amazing young woman. We met at the local coffee shop and she admitted to struggling with her gender identity. She said, "I've never been confused about my gender or my sexuality until my friends started pressuring me." It was an amazing statement, especially in today's world. If she didn't feel safe with me, she never would have said anything like this. The labels children put on children today are killing them. We don't have the category of tomboy like we did in the 1980s. Today, if you're a girl and athletic, you are going to hear that maybe you're a lesbian or even possibly a boy. Now, I'm not making a political or even theological statement here. And I'm certainly not saying that questions around gender and sexuality are bad. I'm just telling you what I'm seeing and how this conversation went.

It is a complicated world and questions around identity are consistently spoken about among teenagers and even by younger children today. This can be a good thing if it isn't happening just among peers. It's another example of how kids need thoughtful and caring adults to help them navigate the world they are growing up in. These issues shouldn't be avoided. I think it's sad when parents have their kids change from a public school to a private school in an attempt to avoid some of these topics. I understand wanting to protect your child, but changing their school won't stop the conversations they and their peers are having around these issues.

Teens need adults engaged in identity formation and positive messaging to teach them that self-worth doesn't rely on how others see them. They need regular time with caring and humble adults who come to the table with no agenda other than to love. Some of this should come through comprehensive and thoughtful conversations and teachings at youth group.

On top of everything else, teens may worry that a less-than-ideal academic performance will lead to being judged by their peers, scolded by their parents, or rejected by their dream schools. Our ministry team had a meeting with all of our high school seniors one night at my house. We sat around the fire pit talking about all of the pressure they were feeling. Some of the students were in tears as they shared about waiting to hear back from the schools where they hoped to be accepted. Even that word, *accepted*, is revealing.

Honestly, I felt frustrated listening to them. So much of what drives these concerns and fears is a lie. You know the lies I mean, right?

- "If I don't get into that school then I'm a failure."
- "If I don't get into that school then I won't get the job that I want to have someday."
- "If I don't get the right job and earn the right salary, I will not be successful."
- "If I don't get into that school then my parents will be embarrassed of me."

How should we respond to these kinds of statements?

I told these kids about how Jesus's name is Immanuel—Hebrew for "God is with us." I told them how he is with them and that not only is he with them, but he really knows them, loves them, and accepts them. He knows what their futures hold, and he thinks it's great! Then I had a college student share with them some of the lies that he had believed when he was younger, and how looking back he wished he hadn't given them so much weight. I felt a simultaneous and collective exhale happen across all of those seniors. That tense back deck around the fire pit instantly became a place of peace. Truth does that to us.

It's just so important that we connect our struggling teens with older peers. We need to have these older young people share their stories of how they've rejected the "perfect college" lie. We can also help our teenagers flourish by giving them opportunities to see a broader perspective and help develop their confidence through things that have nothing to do with academics. We can help parents remember to reassure their kids that academic success is not the prerequisite for love or flourishing.

Then there's the pressure that comes from today's technology. Social media platforms like TikTok, Instagram, and Snapchat have a powerful influence on our lives. Research has shown that despite the ways it connects us, social media actually increases feelings of isolation and depression, especially among teens. Seeing "popularity" quantified in likes and shares can create feelings of jealousy, insecurity, and serious FOMO. Cyberbullying has intensified, especially through the pandemic, and is an increasing problem. With technology also comes exposure to content that may not be appropriate, such as violent pornographic imagery or hate speech. On top of all of this, when teens spend so much time online and so little time interacting face-to-face, they risk not forming the authentic relationships that are vital to social development.

And we as adults need to set good examples. We need to put our own phones away and invest in relationships ourselves. The choices adults make impact the teenagers we care about. When we don't address issues in our own lives, our kids notice and are affected. It reminds me of when I tried to help a teenage boy get off of porn but his parents weren't willing to help at all. I got the feeling that maybe the father was deep into it himself.

It's vital that we show examples of people who are free from the tyranny of media pressure.

Kelsey and I kept our daughter off of social media until she was about sixteen years old. By the time she was allowed to access it she had developed such good habits that it never became a problem. She was used to being present and had developed life patterns that kept her from many of the social media pitfalls. The only issue now is she never looks at her phone, so getting a return text or email from her is harder than trying to get a peace treaty from North Korea. But, my friends, I'll take that over the alternative.

Because the years of adolescence set the stage for adulthood, it's also important to understand and mitigate the unique sources of teen pressure today. Parents, teachers, youth workers, counselors, and anyone who interacts with youth have a responsibility to ensure that teens are set up for the best possible chances of peace and freedom and living lightly. I'm sure the church could be added to the sources of pressure kids feel. But I can tell you this: They've never felt it from Jesus.

Jesus says his burden is light. I love that. I love that the gospel leads to freedom. And I love how Eugene Peterson translates Mathew 11:28-30 in *The Message*:

> "Are you tired? Worn out? Burned out on religion? Come to me. Get away with me and you'll recover your life. I'll show you how to take a real rest. Walk with me and work with me—watch how I do it. Learn the unforced rhythms of grace. I won't lay anything heavy or ill-fitting on you. Keep company with me and you'll learn to live freely and lightly."

Yes. Yes. Yes.

CHAPTER TAKEAWAYS

- Adults should never respond to what teens share by being dismissive or trying to one-up their concerns.
- Teens are under immense pressure from peers, the media and social media, and their parents. They need regular time with adults who come to the table with no agenda other than to love them well.
- As adults, we can show teens what is possible by putting our own phones away, investing in relationships, and addressing the issues in our own lives.

NOTES *from a Mental Health Therapist*

"Self-worth doesn't rely on how others see them." What a profound statement.

I think this is a good reminder for the adults in the room.

For parents: My self-worth is not reliant on how well my teen does on their SATs, or if they are in an AP class, or how they perform in the swim meet. My self-worth is also not determined by others' opinions of me.
For youth workers: My self-worth isn't reliant on whether the numbers keep rising. It isn't even determined by whether I make someone feel better or help a teenager see the bright side of things.

THE ANXIOUS TEEN

For therapists like myself: My self-worth isn't reliant on the number of clients I see each week. Or affected by the number of clients who don't return because they say we aren't a good fit. It is also not determined by someone else's view of the work I do.

That's a good reframe, right? We need to remember that it is unfair if we, as adults, base our own sense of self-worth on the accomplishments of our teens. If we are parents, we need to remember this. If we are youth workers, we need to help the parents we care about remember this. Parents do not have the right to compare their teen to someone else, or compare themselves to others based on what their kid does. It's not evidence of good parenting if a kid gets into the college of *the parent's* dreams.

I have been part of many conversations between parents, teens, and youth workers where the parent wants the youth worker to pick up the baton of helping the kid be successful at x, y, or z. These conversations seem to stem from a parent's frustration or anger and slowly evolve to show the parent's fears being revealed through the list of what-ifs they share about their teens: *What if they don't get good grades? What if they don't into a good school?* The what-ifs can be limitless. When a parent shares one with you, it offers a great starting point for you as a youth worker to help them recognize their own fears.

Maybe the better what-if is, *What if my child does well?* Or, *What if my child were to really enjoy what they are doing?*

The job of parents is to show the love of Jesus through our own actions. It is to see my kid for who they are, help them to grow up feeling loved and secure, and to walk by their side, like Jesus does.

Youth workers get the privilege of fostering relationships with teens without the same level of pressure. Teens need to be able to come to the table, warts and all, and know that they will be seen.

Waiting, Listening, Seeking

Several years ago I was booked to speak on a couple of weekends at a retreat center in the mountains of Northern California. I was told that the kids who attend their retreats were mostly wealthier teens who are also incredibly broken. The director of the camp said that they tended to draw "really smart, secular students," whom he also referred to as "worldly kids."

As the first of these weekends approached, I began to write my talks with that type of kid in mind. I'd bring intellect and humor with a little passion and eventually show them how the gospel not only makes logical sense, but changes everything. As I was preparing, though, there was something else going on behind the scenes. My soul was not well. I had recently been deeply hurt by the church I mentioned in the first chapter. I was feeling beaten up and broken down.

And as you know from earlier, I was still carrying a lot of anger. I was angry at the leadership at that church, angry at coworkers who'd done nothing to help me, angry at my boss. But mostly, I was angry at God.

So there I was writing talks—good talks, solid talks, convincing talks—but I was writing those talks kind of separate from God. I was doing it on my own. Like I said, I wasn't in a good place. I was hurting. And instead of going to God and allowing him to speak to me, heal me, restore me, I was ignoring him and turning to other things to make me feel just a little bit better. Ever done that? It could be food or people or sex or drugs or TV or whatever. Just not God. Definitely not him. He'll make me deal with all of the junk that I'm holding on to, so I'm going to stay away.

THE ANXIOUS TEEN

I arrived at the retreat prepared to give my messages, but down deep I knew I wasn't truly ready. I was feeling dry and disconnected from myself and especially from God. I was getting ready to ask these amazing kids to put down their idols and turn to God in worship, but I was holding idols of pride and pain inside myself. I was ignoring that God was with me in the mess of it all. In my personal life I'd been making decisions that would allow me to avoid dealing with all of the pain. And there I was, Mr. Camp Speaker, professional Christian—or, more accurately, Reverend Fraud.

Each night as I spoke, it felt like my words weren't quite landing. They were pretty-sounding, but they weren't making an impression. They couldn't get below the surface to the heart of each student. Even when I would turn the passion on at key moments, something was left wanting. Heck, *I* was left wanting. I felt numb. The room of students seemed numb. I finished my last talk on the last day and got out of the retreat center as quickly as I could.

I was booked to come back two weekends later. I went home determined to come back for the next retreat spiritually ready. I knew what had happened. My own life had gotten in the way. My words were lifeless and they were disconnected from the Spirit of God. I had done the mental preparation, but I hadn't done any spiritual work. I hadn't dealt with my own sin and my own hurt and brokenness. I hadn't sacrificed anything to get ready.

Right away I began a spiritual fast. The first week I'd pray and fast from caffeine and the second week I'd fast from solid food and pray even harder. I was determined to go to the next retreat with an intimacy with God that I hadn't had the previous weekend. I needed to confess and get right. I needed to ask God to help me to forgive and then join him to live in true freedom. I didn't know if any of these things would affect the kids at the retreat, but they would certainly affect me.

The camp director was right: These kids were rich, smart, broken, and secular. They were also desperate, hungry, and open to meet God, if there actually was a God. I came in ready to introduce them to the One who loves changing people's stories. I gave the exact same talks as the previous weekend, but this time there was more power behind them.

When I got up to speak I didn't worry about how I'd come across. As I stood in front of that room of kids I just felt love and compassion for them. I was seeing them through God's eyes. And the kids in the room were on the edge of their seats every night. Kids were opening their lives to God and confessing. There was a palpable presence of God's Spirit the whole time. The camp director was amazed. "Wow, the content is amazing!" he said. "So much better than the first weekend." Ha! Same talks, bro! They were just brought with a power that didn't come from me.

This two-weekend experiment taught me something: Somehow, my spiritual preparation will impact those I'm ministering to. Our lives are linked in this way. Your spiritual life impacts me, and my spiritual life impacts you. And those we minister to receive the legacy of our own choices. We are all connected.

I meet with youth pastors all of the time who hesitantly and very reluctantly confess that they rarely read the Bible, have quiet times, or pray. And when they do read the Bible, it's to quickly get a proof text for their talk. As far as prayer goes, they rarely do it. In our conversations they've also shared that it's especially rare for them to take time in prayer to listen. Their preparation for a sermon resembles preparing for a presentation in a speech class, rather than what you'd think sermon-writing would look like: waiting, listening, seeking—and then empowerment.

If we are all connected, our spiritual lives impact those around us and those we minister to. If we are not living meaningful spiritual lives, what spiritual legacy are we leaving? What spirit is being transferred from us to others?

We are called to minister to the most addicted, depressed, isolated, anxiety-ridden, fearful, and over-medicated generation in history. And I believe that there is a generation of youth workers who are ready. They are ready to pray without ceasing and do whatever it takes to help this generation of kids become awakened to new life.

EMPOWERED LIFE

Here's the truth to the story of me speaking at that camp. I did what I needed to do to make a difference in the lives of students that second week of camp: I fasted for a couple of weeks and focused on things that got my heart and mind right. But then I came home and slowly went back to my old habits. My old bitterness and anger came back. I couldn't sustain what I'd done before the second weekend. I was like a boxer who trains intensely for a fight, and then after it's over they gain a bunch of weight and slack off. When another fight comes up they train...but afterward they slack off again. This is not a great pattern for a boxer or for a follower of Jesus who's called to in-the-trenches daily work with students.

I spent a couple of years like this, with my practices and time with God roller-coastering all over the place. I'm amazed by the grace of God to use someone like me during those times when I've struggled. Man, he's good! Then I ended up getting help from a counseling student. After that I went on some light medication for a couple of months to take the edge off of my anxiety. Then after about a year of counseling I was in a much better place. Counseling saved me. And yet, even though I was healthy, something was still missing.

Here's where it gets a little weird. This is your warning. Ha!

I was brought up in the charismatic church during the heyday of the Jesus movement. Seeing people worship with passion, give prophetic words, and dance with ribbons felt normal. Well, maybe not the ribbons. I never did like those ribbons.

When I was in second grade, the church pastor's wife prayed for me. When she prayed over me I became overwhelmed with the presence of God's Spirit, and then I began to speak in another language. Yeah, I know, weird. But it gets even more strange. A lady who I had never seen before came running over and said, in a thick accent, that I was speaking in the language of her home country. We were all blown away!

Something similar happened when I was in seventh grade, but this time when I spoke in another language, the pastor who was leading the prayer ministry put the microphone to my mouth and my words went out over the PA system for everyone to hear. As a seventh grader, I was mortified. I swore that I'd never do anything like that again.

Time went by. I studied theology in college at a dispensational school and then I went to two dispensational seminaries. My college and seminaries taught me that, unlike what I'd been told in the charismatic churches of my childhood, we didn't really need the gifts of the Spirit anymore because we had the gifts of the Scriptures.

More years went by. My wife and daughter and I were living in the Northeast. I was working as a youth worker and was just coming out of my own issues with anxiety. I had seen that counselor and gone on medication, yet, as I said, I felt like there was something still missing from my spiritual life.

I began to pray a little prayer each morning. It went something like this: "God, if you'd like to have me speak again in another language, I'd kind of like that. But no pressure."

I prayed that prayer every morning for about a year before I found myself in London visiting a church called Holy Trinity Brompton. I was standing in the balcony of the sanctuary during worship when all of the sudden I was overwhelmed by the power and presence of the Holy Spirit. I began to speak in another language. This was the first time that had happened since I was in seventh grade. I went downstairs and toward the front of the room to be prayed for.

The young man who was assigned to pray for me couldn't have been more than fifteen years old. He asked if he could place his hands on my shoulder. I said yes. He touched me and then spoke again.

"Oh, I have this overwhelming feeling. I sense that God has called you to young people. Is this true?"

THE ANXIOUS TEEN

"Um, yes?"

"I sense that God is going to use you in a greater way, in a more impactful way. God wants to anoint the work of your hands and the words of your mouth in a fresh way for this generation. Do you want this?"

"Um, yes? I mean, yes."

Then he prayed for me, and I felt God's Spirit. That prayer changed me. It led me into a new way of living. A more Christian way of living. A profoundly more spiritual way of living. I didn't become a charismatic, but I definitely became a Trinitarian and I began to daily embrace the empowerment by God's Spirit that I experienced when that young man prayed for me.

God changed me. In doing so he changed my family. He changed our ministry. After that point, when I prayed for kids, it was no longer just something I thought I should do, a religious add-on. Instead it was a close interaction between them, me, and God. This changed my life and my ministry. What we do in our private lives impacts our effectiveness in our public ministry.

For anyone struggling with this thinking or even the theology behind it, let me end with a John Calvin quote:

"Words fail to explain how necessary prayer is and in how many ways the exercise of prayer is profitable. Surely, with good reason, the Heavenly Father affirms that the only stronghold of safety is in calling upon his name."[45]

We can't forget what we're doing here. You can't forget why you're reading this book, even. We have been called to an almost impossible task. On our own, we will fail. Even if we come together in strategy and purpose, we won't solve everything that needs to be solved. We can't fix all that's going on today in the hearts, minds, and souls of these precious young people. We need God to do more than we could do on our own. We need the miraculous to break into the normal.

Recently I came across Psalm 73 and it gripped my heart and mind in a way it never had before. Here it is:

> Whom have I in heaven but you? And earth has nothing I desire besides you. My flesh and my heart may fail, but God is the strength of my heart and my portion forever.
> —Psalm 73:25-26

My hope is that this prayer gets printed on each one of our hearts.

> *God, I desire nothing compared to you. There really isn't anything I long for that compares to you. Even if my heart stops beating, my passion for you never will stop. You are my strength. You are my life. Begin in me what you long to do in the young lives around me.*

CHAPTER TAKEAWAYS

- As youth workers, we have to watch the tendency to go through the motions while ignoring our own struggles and needs. Take the time to care for yourself, do things that are good for you and your faith, and talk to others about your struggles.

- We are all connected. Each of our spiritual lives affects the people around us.

NOTES *from a Mental Health Therapist*

I love Brock's ability to be open and honest about his heart. I am sure that he has never met a stranger, that he will sit and listen with the best of them, and that he will share his heart with those around him.

Brock's story shows how he has grown in his awareness of himself. It is a gift to be able to share about our struggles without claiming them as our whole identity.

Brock was able to heal from his hurt and anger caused by his experience at the church he worked for. He found that he didn't need to go back and confront those who had hurt him in order to heal. His healing came through bringing his anger and hurt to God.

Holding onto anger can impact our emotional well-being. The anger we hold onto impacts our relationships. If you've ever had a bad breakup, you likely know the way it can affect how you interact with your next partner. We have a label for this: baggage. We sometimes carry our baggage from past hurts like a medal of honor, and we use it to defend our behavior: "Of course I check his phone, I've been cheated on."

Unexpressed anger is linked to both depression and anxiety. Teens who are feeling depression often express it through anger and "acting out" behaviors. In a 2012 study published in the journal *Cognitive Behavior Therapy*, researchers found that "anger can exacerbate symptoms of generalized anxiety disorder."[46]

Holding onto anger isn't good for our emotional health, but neither is jumping to forgiveness without actually being ready. Don't be hasty to forgive if you aren't yet in a place to do so. You are allowed to feel hurt, anger, or sadness because of someone else's actions. Acknowledge and allow for your feelings. Brock had every right to feel anger toward the people of the church he worked for; they had hurt him.

When you are ready to forgive, ask yourself if you need to have a conversation with the person you are forgiving: *Do I need this to be free of any held resentment?* It is okay to not have a conversation. There is a common misconception that to forgive someone we must talk it out. That is not true. We can grant forgiveness without discussion. Sometimes talking things through is not possible because the other person may be unwilling or unavailable. Sometimes a discussion would only fall on deaf ears. It is okay to recognize this and choose not to go there.

Another question to ask yourself is, *Did I play a part in what happened?* This can be a tough one. Taking ownership can be difficult, but will go a long way in your healing. There might even come a time when you need to forgive yourself.

Like Brock, you might also find that you are harboring anger and resentment.

If that's the case, it could be time to get outside help. This can be especially true if you are unwilling or unable to let what happened go. Seek therapy, talk to a trusted friend, spend time with God.

Re-embracing Meditation

The meditation-and-the-brain research has been rolling in steadily for a number of years now. This research shows that meditation can not only bring peace, but can rewire the brain—the same groovy brains we were just learning about a couple of chapters ago. Scientists are discovering that meditation slows the aging process in the brain, reduces stressful thoughts, alleviates depression and anxiety, improves concentration, and significantly improves learning.[47]

And here's the cool thing: Meditation is biblical. I believe it will not only help you as a youth worker, but could be a game changer for teenagers today. The ancient practice of meditation can be part of how our students move through their struggles toward healing and wholeness.

I know, I know, some of you are cringing right now. Your mind immediately went to transcendental meditation, and you're skeptical. Maybe you're picturing the Beatles with the Dalai Lama. Stick with me. I believe there's something here for you.

Because here's the thing: There are many forms of meditation, and meditation can help us connect with God in a meaningful way.

One of the greatest discoveries of my life is that the Creator of the Universe tends to whisper. When I was young in my faith, I expected God to speak to me with a flare. Cue the smoke machine, the lights, me with my shoes off on a mountaintop. I expected God to communicate through dramatic, hype-laden speeches. I wanted him to show up and kick down the door and speak to me in a deep James Earl Jones voice. "Brock, I am your father."

Yes, occasionally there are loud, obvious moments that I love: the walking on water, the fire from heaven, and the skipping out of the grave. The truth, though, is that God tends to prefer the slow, the quiet, and the unspectacular. We expect thunder and lightning and dazzle, but instead he sidles up in the twilight to whisper in our ears. God whispers. Once I learned this, it revolutionized my relationship with God.

In 1 Kings 19, the prophet Elijah has been told to "go out and stand on the mountain in the presence of the Lord, for the Lord is about to pass by." And after he does, sure enough, something happens: "Then a great and powerful wind tore the mountains apart and shattered the rocks before the Lord, but the Lord was not in the wind. After the wind, there was an earthquake, but the Lord was not in the earthquake."

Then, the unexpected occurs: God *quietly whispers* to Elijah. This is the voice of God.

God is not in the noise. He is in the quiet.

Think about our world. It's loud, noisy, fast, distracted, anxious. It's like Elijah's violent wind and earthquake. Our students have had a screen in their faces from the time they were placed in a car seat in the back of the minivan. Our world is a really difficult place to hear a whisper. And yet that's how God approaches us. As Richard Rohr writes,

> …he comes disguised as our life, which seems to be the last place we want God to be. It's all too ordinary, mundane, fleshy, and unspiritual. It is just 'me' and just 'you' and just daily life. It is both the perfect hiding place and the perfect revelation place for the Holy One.[48]

I love the concept of the *with-ness* of God. I don't think that it's an actual word, but let's make it one. *With-ness*. God is not an invisible sky fairy. God is a universal presence and as Colossians and Hebrews both say, he is filling all things and in all things and pulling everything forward. God is in here, in there, in everywhere. He is with you and with them and with all. His with-ness can change everything. And a life of meditation is a life attentive to him.

I think a lot of us miss noticing just how much God is right with us, in all things, always. In seminary I was taught God is so holy that he cannot tolerate sin in his presence. Well, if that's the case, then the incarnation is impossible. The truth is that God is with us *always*. God took on the very flesh of sinful humans, hung out with and touched sinful people, and as Paul said, even *became* sin so that sin might be done away with through his death. God's holiness does not shun sin, it runs to it and transforms it. God's light does not hide from darkness, it shines within it, causing darkness to cease. God is present with us, in the midst of the noise, the distractions, the busyness, the sinning, the darkness, the anger, the doubt, and the anxiety. This is God's with-ness, and we need to help our students tune in to him.

So as people who love kids who are struggling to be present, kids who live in a world that is not helping them be aware of the with-ness of God, what can we do? How can we help them sense and hear God? If God is always with them, speaking in a whisper, how can we help them tune into that reality?

This is where meditation can help.

I remember being a very young youth worker one of the first times I had seen anyone lead a time of meditation with students. I had asked our pastor to come and speak to our kids on anything he wanted to. I was expecting him to drop some wisdom on our students or do a time of Q&A, but instead he came in and said, "I thought instead of me talking all night we'd let God speak to each one of us."

I thought inside, *Um, what?*

He went on and told the students that God speaks to us through the Scriptures but also through our emotions, through our thoughts, and also through images and visions. He said that we just needed to make space for God to speak. We needed to turn on the quiet and listen. Then he asked us all to get comfortable, close our eyes, take a deep breath in, and be still and open to listen.

Now I have to tell you, I was skeptical. Honestly, I thought this was probably a waste of time. Little did I know. After about four or five minutes of silence he said, "When you're ready, open your eyes and look at me."

Over the next minute or so they all began to look at the pastor. "Okay, what were you sensing from God?" he asked. A few kids all had reflected on the same passage of Scripture, and a couple saw the same picture in their minds, which happened to be connected to the Scripture passage. Many others said they were overcome by God's presence and had an overwhelming sense of peace. If there had been a skeptical kid in the room, that experience cemented their belief in a present and loving God. This was a huge lesson for me!

Afterward this pastor told me the secret to leading people in times of meditation. He said that he had spent all day praying for that time with students. He prepared for it spiritually, and as he was preparing he sensed something specific: that God wanted to show the students that he is with them and that he is longing to work in their personal lives and in their everyday. All of that happened before the time of meditation. Again, what a lesson for me!

In college I was encouraged to read *Practicing the Presence of God* by Brother Lawrence. It's an amazing little book that packs a big punch. Brother Lawrence was a man of humble beginnings who discovered a great secret of living in the kingdom of God here on Earth. He writes all about practicing the presence of God in a never-ending way. He writes about doing life with God. Cleaning dishes with God, scrubbing the floors with God, serving the poor with God. Just everyday living in the midst of God's amazing presence. Waking up each day with an expectant heart. "What's next, Papa?" (Romans 8:15, MSG).

When I was in high school one of our youth leaders challenged us to do something similar. He said, "Try to pray this week without ceasing." I remember taking it to heart, but to be honest, I didn't know what to pray. I didn't know how to pray. In the midst of my uncertainty over how to do what our youth leader encouraged, I remembered a time when I'd been really sick as a little boy. My dad would come into my room, rub my head, and just pray over and over again the name "Jesus."

"Jesus. Jesus. Jesus…
Jesus, heal my boy. Jesus. Jesus. Jesus…"

I remember listening to him praying the name of Jesus and how it soothed me and helped me fall asleep. Jesus's name brought me peace. So that is what I decided to do when our youth leader issued the challenge. I'd walk in the hallways at school and go to class and play basketball and do my homework, all the while praying Jesus's name over and over again.

As I did this, something amazing happened. I began to become aware of God's with-ness.

I've kept up this habit of praying all the time for about thirty-five years now. That's crazy to think about! And it all started with a youth worker calling me into a life of devotion and connectedness. A life of meditation.

Many times this is where I begin with kids, and many kids have taken me up on the challenge. I ask them what would happen if we thought about our lives as a never-ending conversation with God. This has become a game-changer for so many, just as it was for Brother Lawrence, just as it was for me. It's difficult to look at porn when you're habitually doing life with Jesus. It's difficult to do anything disconnected from God when you're praying without ceasing.

What I've tried to do is to embrace a life of meditation myself and invite students into it with me. Meditation, in this sense, just means being attentive to God. It is one way we "keep seeking the things above where Christ is" (Colossians 3:1). But it's also leaning into and focusing on his Word.

It says in the Bible, "This book of the law shall not depart from your mouth, but you shall meditate on it day and night, so that you may be careful to do according to all that is written in it. For then you will make your way prosperous, and then you will have good success" (Joshua 1:8).

THE ANXIOUS TEEN

I love the practice of Lectio Divina because it is incorporating what Joshua and some of the Psalms call us to: meditating on God's Word. Lectio Divina is a slow, rhythmic reading and praying of a Scripture passage. You pick a passage and read it. Notice what arises within you as you read it. Then you read it again and then one more time, noticing what words and phrases grab your heart and what feelings arise. You respond to God about whatever is stirring within as you read and pray through the passage. Finally, you rest and let God respond and speak to you. There are so many sites online that give you a practical, step-by-step process of how to do Lectio Divina yourself or lead a group through it, so I won't get into that now. The important thing is to give practices like these a try—because man do we need to get back into mediating on God's Word!

The Scriptures tell us this: "Blessed is the man who walks not in the counsel of the wicked, nor stands in the way of sinners, nor sits in the seat of scoffers; but his delight is in the law of the Lord, and on his law he meditates day and night" (Psalm 1:1-2).

The goal is to not just teach students and give them information, but to show them how to live and move and have their being in God. Our youth ministries must move into involvement and participation, allowing for collaborative and transformative experiences that help each person grow into a devoted, connected, empowered, peace-filled follower of Jesus.

As we know, our students are looking desperately for belonging. As they learn to cultivate meditation into their lives, they will find what their hearts and minds have been craving since their birth.

I enjoyed watching the film series *The Chosen*, a historical drama based on Jesus's life. I was struck by how devoted to God the young disciples of Jesus were. Many of them were devoted before they even met Jesus. As Jews, episode after episode showed that their very lives were meditative. Even the flawed character Peter would wake up every morning and habitually pray to his God. I did something similar. About ten years ago I put into my phone reminders to pray. Ever since, three times a day, my phone buzzes telling me to keep pursuing God.

I remember a saying I used to hear a lot as a kid. It was about people who were "too heavenly minded to be any earthly good." But in this anxious, stressed, uncertain world, we could all benefit from being more kingdom-of-heaven minded. I have benefited from counseling and even from medication at times. There are a lot of resources that can help when we are struggling. But more than anything else, I know that what has brought peace into my life is the power and presence of God.

I love these words from Jonathan Edwards, used to describe a particular encounter with the power and wonder of creation:

> And as I was walking there [in his father's pasture] and looking upon the sky and clouds, there came into my mind so sweet a sense of the glorious majesty and grace of God as I know not how to express. . . . The appearance of everything was altered; there seemed to be, as it were, a calm, sweet cast, or appearance of divine glory, in almost everything. God's excellency, his wisdom, his purity and love, seemed to appear in everything; in the sun, moon, and stars, in the clouds and blue sky, in the grass, flowers, trees, in the water and all nature; which used greatly to fix my mind. I often used to sit and view the moon for a long time, and in the day spent much time in viewing the clouds and sky, to behold the sweet glory of God in these things; in the meantime singing forth, with a low voice, my contemplations of the Creator and Redeemer. And scarce anything among all the works of nature was so sweet to me as thunder and lightning; formerly nothing had been so terrible to me. Before, I used to be uncommonly terrified with thunder, and to be struck with terror when I saw a thunder-storm rising; but now, on the contrary, it rejoiced me. I felt God, if I may so speak, at the first appearance of a thunder-storm; and used to take the opportunity at such times to fix myself in order to view the clouds and see the lightnings play and hear the majestic and awful voice of God's thunder, which oftentimes was exceedingly entertaining, leading me to sweet contemplations of my great and glorious God. While thus engaged it always seemed natural for me to sing or chant forth my meditations, or to speak my thoughts in soliloquies with a singing voice.[49]

THE ANXIOUS TEEN

I love his passion. This is what I want to emulate when I talk about time spent with God, about meditation, about transformation, about peace. This is what I want to invite our students into. This is the deep stuff that kids are longing for.

I've also learned from the words of John Stott, one of the greatest Christian leaders of the twentieth century. In 2005, *Time* magazine ranked him in the world's top 100 most influential people. Toward the end of his life Stott was asked if he would change anything if he were able to live his life over again. He paused thoughtfully and answered, "I would pray more."[50] This was the response of someone who, while at university, set his alarm clock to 6 a.m. for daily prayer. In later life, he got up even earlier, setting his alarm for 5 a.m. Stott kept a notebook of situations and people to pray about. He began and ended each day in prayer.

I've also learned from a Muslim friend and neighbor. He used to be a Christian, but he converted as a young man and we've developed a fun relationship with each other. From time to time we have the occasional insightful and vulnerable conversation. One afternoon we were both outside our houses and he asked me about our church. After I told him about it he looked at me and said, "I think one of the main reasons I became a Muslim was because I found Christianity to be so very unspiritual." I smiled and nodded. "I know, right? So many people following the most spiritual person ever, Jesus, and they've turned it into a discipleship class that's disconnected from the Spirit of God." He looked at me and said, "Yes!"

I said, "You know, lately I've been meeting more and more followers of Jesus who are praying without ceasing. They are spending their lives trying to be connected to his Spirit and it is changing them. God is becoming real to them." He was intrigued. "If my church were like that, I never would have left," he said.

The noise of our lives keeps us from being connected to God. I love what Chuck Swindoll says about this:

> In place of our exhaustion and spiritual fatigue, God will give us rest. All He asks is that we come to Him...that we spend a while

thinking about Him, meditating on Him, talking to Him, listening in silence, occupying ourselves with Him—totally and thoroughly lost in the hiding place of His presence.[51]

I've seen God show up and do the spectacular. Healings and spooky and wonderful God stuff. But he mostly whispers, so we must help our students—and ourselves—slow down, be still, wait, and listen for him.

CHAPTER TAKEAWAYS

- Meditation is biblical. This ancient practice can be part of how our students move toward healing and wholeness.

- Meditation can help us hear the often quiet whisper of God's voice in our lives.

- Making space in our youth ministries for silence, reflection, and meditation can be awkward at first. That's okay. It doesn't mean it's not worthwhile or isn't working. Awkwardness is often a part of trying something new.

NOTES *from a Mental Health Therapist*

It's extremely challenging to help our teens to slow down. To encourage them to be still and to listen. They are likely to say they have too much to do, they don't have time, they don't want to. And yet there are immense benefits that come from doing a slower, more thoughtful pace. We can help our teens by introducing them to practices like mindfulness meditation.

"Being mindful" simply means being fully present in the here and now. Mindfulness is challenging for a lot of people because we are so focused on doing what we have to do. Our schedules are so full that we are constantly trying to keep up, get things done, and not forget anything. For teens there is the added stress of wanting to be accepted and not be left out. There is a lot of pressure filling up the quiet spaces of our lives.

Though it might sound intimidating, mindfulness meditation simply means allowing yourself to spend time being aware of what is going on inside and around you without judgment or interpretation. It is the practice of noticing what is happening and what you are feeling. It is not about trying to change your feelings, but simply recognizing and allowing what is happening to happen. It is a great way to reduce stress.

The first step of mindfulness meditation is to observe the present moment. Although this sounds easy it can be difficult. The goal is not to quiet the mind (like in other forms of meditation), the goal is to become aware of the things around you right now. You can do an internal scan of how your body is feeling, both physically and emotionally. Again, this scan is not to make note of problems and make changes—it is simply about noticing.

Second, recognize what is going on around you in the environment. While observing the present moment you can bring your attention back to your breathing.

Over time you'll become more able to notice what is going on inside and around you without judgment or interpretation, which will allow you to experience peace and hear the still, small voice of God in the midst of whatever is happening in your life.

Grounding is another important tool that can benefit us all. Grounding means anchoring ourselves in the present—reminding ourselves not to focus on what's next on our list, but to sit and be in the current moment. A great way to feel grounded is to actually feel the solidness of the ground beneath you. Sometimes when I know it would be helpful for me to ground myself, I take off my shoes and walk in the grass, paying attention to how it feels.

Tips for mindfulness practices for youth workers and students:

Allow time: Mindfulness takes time. At first, taking any time for mindfulness meditation might feel very difficult. That is okay. You might feel resistance toward the idea of even trying. That's okay too. Things will change as it becomes a more regular and familiar part of your day.

Observe the present moment: Although this sounds easy, it can be quite difficult. The goal is not to quiet the mind (like it is in transcendental meditation). The goal in mindfulness meditation is to become aware without immediately reacting.

Wounded Healers

A couple of years ago I attended a seminar on sexuality and gender called "Being Human" given by Sam Fergusson and John Yates.[52] They began the seminar by saying that every single one of us is sexually broken. All of us. Yes, even your grandma. This reminded me of how the Anglican Church begins their services with the Prayer of Confession. This kind of corporate prayer is a way of admitting that we all are starting from the same point. Each one of us needs God's grace for things we've done and for things we've left undone.

From time to time over the years I've attended AA meetings. I'll go with a friend who regularly attends or I'll just pop in by myself. It's not that I have a problem with alcohol, it's just that I'm desperate for the vulnerability that's on display in those gatherings. In my experience they've invited me in and said I'm welcome to observe. I leave those meetings feeling connected and encouraged and hope-filled.

> "Hi, my name is Brock Morgan and I'm a mess and I'm desperate for this community."

I bring up these stories of vulnerability and confession because I think we need a lot more of them. For so long, churches—especially the ones I have experienced—ministered from a place of strength or success. I have heard so many testimonies that end with everything tied up in a beautiful bow: "Then I gave my life to Jesus and, well, I've never struggled again."

THE ANXIOUS TEEN

Pastors get up and talk about their successful prayer life with never a hint of struggle. They'll share how their marriage is perfect and how sexy their spouse is. They'll talk about how God speaks to them in an almost audible voice.

No long ago I was listening to a random podcast and I heard a pastor being interviewed about all the wounds they've received from church people. But he shared it all in a way that made it look like he had been impervious to any feelings about it all. He completely skimmed over the fact that he'd had a couple of breakdowns over the years as a result. Now maybe he didn't want to make a big deal out of it all and focus on all of the trauma he went through, but what ended up being communicated was a shallow, inauthentic telling. He shared in a way that might give you the feeling that God had never gone silent on him and that he had never really struggled to have faith in the midst of all the horrific pain. Sitting there and listening, I knew better.

As a kid growing up in that "strength culture," I never felt like I could be honest about my own weaknesses. Secretly, I thought I didn't have what it took to be a follower of Jesus, because I knew I didn't have it all together.

This kind of church culture creates a bunch of pretenders. We can see this in the Bible when Jesus confronts church leaders, people who look like they have it all together on the outside but have filthy inner lives. This is what the Bible calls hypocrisy, and religion is a breeding ground for it. In my life growing up, it meant that I became an expert at hiding my weaknesses and struggles.

Many of our students are going through the same thing. When they begin to struggle or have questions or doubts or fears, instead of getting help or inviting someone into the journey with them, they hide. They've absorbed that they're supposed to highlight strength and success over honest vulnerability.

Kelsey and I have a rule in our home that we try to follow: We never struggle alone. We don't hide or isolate. We choose to struggle together. This means we regularly ask each other how we're doing. We have family meetings where we model appropriate confession. We say out loud what our struggles are, what fears or anxieties we can't seem to shake. We invite each other into the struggle. We've brought this rule into our youth ministry as well.

This practice reminds us that struggle is inevitable. We will *all* struggle. We *all* have weaknesses. Every single one of us sometimes doubts or lusts or fears or lacks faith. Hiding our struggles not only hurts ourselves; it hurts the larger community. Any time we're not being real and open and honest, it hurts everybody else. When we bring the struggle to the table, we all get in on it. We not only get to rally around the person struggling, but we gain wisdom from the struggle together.

An amazing tenth grade guy started coming to our youth group about a year ago. Initially he was super friendly and outgoing, but I noticed him gradually withdrawing: rarely smiling, no longer sharing in his small group—it's like there was a darkness coming over him. When I mentioned it to his mom, she told me he'd been struggling at home with his temper. He'd also started hiding in his bedroom and avoiding everyone whenever he was home. When I asked if I could get together with him she said it would be great, but doubted he'd share anything with me about what was really going on.

We met up at Starbucks and after a couple sips of my iced chai latte I jumped right in. "Dude, what's going on? Recently I've been feeling that you are struggling." He replied with something that made me so happy. He said, "Well, I know we're not supposed to hide what's going on in our lives from each other…" He might not normally have wanted to share, but he knew the rule we'd brought from our home into our youth group: We never struggle alone. He knew he was safe to share, and that struggling together was an expectation. He began to tell me what had been plaguing him. When you have a culture like this in the DNA, kids catch it. It becomes their liberation.

When we acknowledge that struggles are a part of life to be shared and faced, not avoided or hidden, it causes a massive cultural shift. Pretending isn't an option when vulnerability is on display. This vulnerability demonstrates strength, not weakness. This is the great reversal that we get to help create.

THE ANXIOUS TEEN

"Hi, my name is Brock Morgan and I'm really struggling with my faith."

Many of us are afraid to let ourselves, our leaders, our students, or our parents become truly vulnerable. We're afraid that sharing these stories will cause others to feel better about their own compromises or shortcomings. It's like a pastor who is afraid to preach about God's love, grace, and forgiveness in case it teaches people not to fear God enough and they'll stop toeing the line. Fear. Control.

This kind of fear and control is called legalism. Legalism leads to hiding and hiding leads to perversion—it's a vicious cycle. When I keep my sin or my struggle secret, that sucker turns on me and becomes incredibly powerful and can become embedded into my life.

What would it look like for our students to realize that they weren't alone in their struggles, and that their weaknesses were something that could be shared, acknowledged, and faced within a loving community? That this was the norm. What if we ministered to them from a place of vulnerability rather than a place of strength?

About fifteen years ago I made a decision. I would not show only strength and competence from up front but I would lead and preach and minister from a place of weakness. Like Paul, I would boast about my struggles. The goal was not to give people some ideas about how to sin really big. The idea was to minister from a place of vulnerability.

First, I had to stop telling kids how my relationship with Jesus *had changed* me. Instead, I'd tell them how my relationship with Jesus *was changing* me. I made it clear that I was still in process, still desperate for God's Spirit to work in me, still longing for his peace and joy and love to break into my life. I'd tell them that I needed God just as much today as the day I first met him.

Second, I put our kids' stories on display, having them share from their own lives in a more open and less polished way. It didn't matter that they were still in the middle of whatever they were going through. We don't only need to hear stories of how someone has successfully navigated something hard.

We also need to hear stories of what it's like in the middle of the mess and the questions and the difficulty. I know I need this, and our students do too.

We did a series at youth group all about doubt. When we asked students to share, I made sure we didn't ask only kids who had success stories of how they used to doubt and now were doing great. No! I also had kids share who were in the midst of questioning and in the midst of their doubt. This might make some of you nervous. But it was incredibly awesome and helpful and relatable to hear where they were in the midst of some of life's big questions.

I picked tender-hearted doubting kids, the soft skeptics who really wanted to know the truth for themselves. They were hungry for it and this hunger impacted the other kids. These students sharing about their doubts were curious. They wanted to know more. They were struggling, and open about their struggle. Hearing their stories was deeply meaningful, and it changed the course of our series and the conversations that came out of it.

This decision to have students share more vulnerably enabled better conversations. It led to open dialogue among our group, and helped shift our youth group culture to one where truth-seeking was the norm—as opposed to appearing to know all of the answers and have everything together. This shift was not only powerful in the lives of the students who were listening, but also in the lives of those who shared. In the midst of doubt, faith was strengthened because vulnerability was displayed. Our honest conversations led us into deeper things.

A couple of years ago we did another series, this time focused on anxiety and peace. Again we had teenagers in our group give testimony to their ongoing fears and anxieties and worries. They shared how they felt coming into the youth room and how it sometimes created social anxiety inside of them. They shared the overwhelming pressure they felt about school. They talked about how desperate they were for God to give them peace.

Again, their vulnerable sharing was powerful. As they gave voice to what so many in our group were also experiencing, the kids who shared felt supported, empowered, and less alone (some of them for the first time in their lives). This opened the door to more kids confessing that they also needed help. That they felt plagued by anxiety. Out of this came amazing times of prayer and support.

Here is what this kind of vulnerability does: it calls each one of us to step into our calling as a "wounded healer."

"Hi, my name is Brock Morgan and I've been wounded."

The term "wounded healer" was coined by psychiatrist Carl Jung. The idea is that someone who has or is currently experiencing pain can be a powerful presence for those who are struggling. That pain or that struggle gets redeemed right in front of their eyes. This is what we were seeing in our ministry. All of the sudden a student with anxiety could see how God was using their battle with anxiety to give help and hope to others. They could see how what they'd gone through had given them wisdom and experience and enabled them to empathize with others better.

When you are helping someone, your own wounds miraculously end up becoming a gift. This is why at the beginning of the book I said that my own struggle with anxiety has become my superpower.

The idea of the wounded healer has helped shape my concept of student leadership. I've hated how youth ministry has been so much about the adults in charge. In many youth groups, adults lead the games and the mixers, we preach, we head up the small groups, do the announcements, and act in skits—all while the kids sit and watch the show.

Think about the difference between the average youth group and a high school. At school kids are doing the activities, putting together the year-book, leading the assemblies, playing on the field, running the sound and lights for the play, and being the stage manager. Then they come to youth group and they might see a kid on stage helping lead worship, but that's pretty much it. An adult gives the talk. The students don't see this but often on our way home we ask our spouse, "So what did you think about my talk? Was it good? Was I funny?" Like this thing is about us.

And then we wonder why kids quit coming by the end of tenth grade. Why do they stop? Because they're not really needed, not really being used, and they've already heard you tell that story at least four times. When we make youth group about us, we're communicating that we believe in the strength model. We believe it's got to be perfect and sound awesome.

"Hi, my name is Brock Morgan and I'm a control freak."

Any healthy future for youth ministry will require us to help our teens see how needed they are. How gifted they are. How their struggles, their anxieties, and their mistakes can be redeemed and how God can bring good out of really hard and difficult things. What the enemy meant for evil, God can use for good. I believe we are called to invite our teenagers to join us in being wounded healers.

A while back I got a phone call from a teenage guy who was overwhelmed with debilitating anxiety. He was an incredible athlete but had been struggling on the playing field. He was also a great student, but was overwhelmed by the fear of failure. It got to the point where he was having a hard time coping with daily life. He asked if we could meet, and I told him that I'd of course love to. Before we hung up I asked if it would be okay if I brought one of our students with me.

The student I had in mind had not only been through similar things, but had recently turned a corner. He was still struggling in some ways, but I felt like God could use this student's story to help this other young man. When we got together later I had the privilege of watching this wounded healer minister to his peer. It was one of the most amazing times of ministry I've ever had. Since then, I have been able to do the same thing with other students. They get to see, firsthand, how the pain they have gone through, and may even be continuing to go through, can be used by God. They can see God use their life and their whole story—not just their successes and strengths.

"Hi, my name is _____, and I'm a wounded healer."

When I first experienced debilitating anxiety, we were beginning to see many kids going through the same thing. I remember counseling them and listening to their stories. Initially I was afraid to tell them about my own struggle. I was afraid that I would be viewed as weak. I also think I had some bad theology around suffering and sin that led me to believe that if I told them about my current struggle it might validate that they were fine the way they were—or more likely, that it would somehow communicate that if I, as a Jesus-follower, was struggling, then the gospel must not be that powerful. Plus, I was definitely afraid of my bosses finding out. I'd had seen a friend escorted out of his youth worker position because of something similar.

After about a year of listening to my kids' heartbreaking stories while struggling internally with my own anxiety, I finally came clean to them. I talked about it in our group one night. I remember the kids being shocked. I overheard one kid telling some of his friends that he couldn't believe that I had shared that with them. But they weren't disappointed. They valued the vulnerability I'd shown by opening my life up to them.

Now, we have to use wisdom when we share our story. Please don't be an idiot up front trying to get attention. There are ways of sharing that don't give students ideas or glorify anyone's sin, or make it about us—we need to be discerning about how and what we share. But we can afford to be more vulnerable. Our students need us to be.

What this vulnerability did in our group was bring momentum. It made others feel safer to share. It helped us connect. And it brought us smack dab to the middle of the gospel. The overwhelming good news is that God loves us and he is with us and he is for us. He longs for us to walk freely and lightly in his power. He's with us in the middle of our doubts and our fears—he can handle it! And man, that's really good news.

Every one of us is broken. We can relate when a kid tells us that they don't trust the church, that it's not a safe place. Churches are imperfect, and we've experienced that ourselves, sometimes with deeply painful results. We know what it's like to be gripped by fear: fear of losing our job or status, fear of what people might think, fear of the future, fear of the unknown. But take heart!

Our stories are not valuable only once we've overcome every obstacle. They are powerful in the beginning and the middle, too. There is power in our vulnerability and in our weakness.

When I enter into that vulnerable place with other people, it reveals a few things. First, it shows others that the only way to overcome brokenness is to lay it bare. It no longer has a hold on us when we confess to ourselves, to God, and to each other. Second, it reveals this foundational truth: I need Jesus. No matter my age or my stage, I will always need the love and forgiveness he offers. My life depends on him. And last, it gives others the opportunity to minister.

My wife once shared with her small group of squirrely middle school girls her frustration over a recurring, debilitating ankle injury. She was emotional as she asked, "Can you girls pray for me?" In that moment of vulnerability, those young girls leaned into the power of prayer for the first time. Multiple girls prayed out loud, without being coerced, as tears flowed down Kelsey's cheeks. "I sensed God's power and peace, but mostly I felt his sheer enjoyment of those girls," she said afterward. If we don't share our moments of weakness with our kids, they may never experience God using them like this.

"Hi, my name is Jesus, and I'm a wounded healer."

Jesus is the ultimate wounded healer. He was wounded and bruised, and by his stripes we are healed. We have to learn from him and live like him.

Have you ever been in trouble with the leadership in your church? Well, Jesus knows exactly what that's like because he was constantly criticized by church leadership.

Have you wrestled with doubt and overwhelming questions like, "God, where are you?" Well, Jesus can relate to you: "Father, why have you forsaken me?"

Have you ever gotten into trouble because of legalism? I did recently, from some older folks who weren't happy that I'd done a fundraiser at our church on a Sunday. Well, Jesus gets that too.

THE ANXIOUS TEEN

Have you ever lost a loved one to an untimely death? Well, Jesus knows the pain of that as well. He experienced friends dying. He knows the pain of loss.

Each of us has gone through bouts of fear and anxiety. Well, so did Jesus. Some Scriptures even tell us that he sweated blood from his pores because of the tremendous anxiety he experienced before his death. He didn't hide from this, but vulnerably invited his friends into the pain of that moment, pleading with them to stay up with him and pray.

When he told his followers that they would face major persecution, he promised them that he would never leave them or forsake them. Those were not empty words. He knew what it was like to be left, and he'd felt the pain of being forsaken. He was not about to let them go through that all alone. He would always be with them, even through the turmoil, the loss, and the pain.

And here's the cool thing: What Jesus did for his followers, they would get to do for others. The Spirit of Jesus would empower them to join the suffering and bring a presence and a hope that they never would have received otherwise. As wounded healers we get to be part of the blessing and gift of empathy. This is what following Jesus can look like in the lives of anxious teens and it's why I so desperately want Jesus to continue to change me.

> *"Hi, my name is Brock and I really want to be like Jesus. Because only when I am like Jesus can I help hurting kids be like Jesus, too."*

CHAPTER TAKEAWAYS

- Many of our students—and many of us as youth workers—have absorbed the idea that we should highlight our strengths and hide our weaknesses and struggles. This way of thinking hurts rather than helps us.

- Struggle is inevitable. We all have weaknesses. When we struggle together we can help each other, learn from each other, and draw from one another's wisdom.

- Our ministries will change for the better when we minister from a place of vulnerability rather than a place of strength. There are healthy ways for youth workers to share about their struggles in their ministries, and encourage students to do the same.

- We all need to hear stories of the hard times: what it's like in the middle of the mess and the questions and the difficulty. When students are able to share their doubts and their vulnerabilities, it benefits their entire youth group and entire community.

NOTES *from a Mental Health Therapist*

There is this notion in the therapy world that you can't take your client deeper into their woundedness unless you are willing to go deeper into yours. In other words, you can't take a client to a place you aren't willing to go yourself.

A few years ago I taught a master's-level student. She had a client who was grieving the death of a parent, and my student was struggling with how to help. I asked my student, "Can you imagine what it would feel like to have your father die?" She didn't like that question, and she couldn't go there. She was not able to sit with her client in the pain of losing a parent.

To help others heal in their pain we need to sit in that pain.

There is something so healing about sitting in the depth of your own pain, knowing that it isn't too big to bear for the person sitting next to you.

When I am sitting with someone in that depth, I hold onto Jesus. Without Jesus too much of our humanness gets in the way, and we can revert to dismissing the pain, trying to return to happiness as quickly as possible.

We need to remember that Jesus is in that pain with us.

I struggle with knowing that the wounds in my story are a gift. I sometimes doubt that God will use my hurts for good. I sometimes wish I didn't have those hurts and didn't know that depth of pain. But I believe that with Jesus, I can help others.

THE ANXIOUS TEEN

I strive to be a wounded healer.

For those who aren't wounded, you can still learn to sit in the discomfort of someone else's angst. Allow yourself to listen and be present with them, to feel uncomfortable without trying to make it go away. Allow yourself to sit quietly while all the feels bubble up. Remember that you don't need to come up with answers or give advice.

Just breathe.

Abba (Inhale)
I belong to you (Exhale)

> *"Hi, my name is Hallie. I have been wounded, and I strive to be a wounded healer."*

Theology and Fear

One of my earliest fears was that my parents would leave and never come back. I know that may sound weird, but my parents were in a Christian rock band that kept them on the road for much of the year. I traveled with them a bunch, but there were also times when they'd leave me and my older sister and head out for a month at a time.

A month is a long time for a little guy to be away from his parents. When my parents were in town, we'd go to a church as a family. This is kind of embarrassing to say, but I was that kid who would cry at drop-off for Sunday school. I legitimately thought my parents might skip town and I'd be stuck for the rest of my life with people I didn't really know in that God-awful classroom that smelled like glue.

Of course my parents never did abandon me. I was just too darn cute for that.

There are many fears that most teenagers have:

- fear of not doing well in school
- fear of disasters like tornadoes, hurricanes, or wildfires
- fear of their parents divorcing
- fear of experiencing peer rejection or not fitting in
- fear of missing out
- fear of not getting into the college of their choice
- fear of a mass shooting

THE ANXIOUS TEEN

But beyond those fears there are many other fears, and some of them cause teenagers major anxiety. Sometimes that anxiety moves beyond the ordinary to become an irrational fear.

A phobia is an extreme, irrational fear of or aversion to something. Usually, the person experiencing the phobia is in little to no actual danger. Phobias are classified as anxiety disorders.[53]

More and more kids are experiencing fears that have become debilitating. Many kids who have a phobia of, let's say, large crowds will walk into a youth room and immediately begin having some symptoms:

- Feeling nauseous or faint
- Sweating, nervous shaking, and blushing
- Sensation of choking and shortness of breath
- Numbness
- Chills or hot flashes
- Chest pain or tightness
- Increased heart rate
- Dizziness
- Confusion and disorientation

When someone with a phobia of large crowds walks into a room full of peers they don't know, their body responds like it's a life-threatening scenario. A teenager feeling this way might stand against the back wall and put on the "don't come over here" vibe or hide behind their cell phone, their only source of comfort.

I love being the greeter at the youth room on Wednesday evenings and welcoming students in. It's my favorite! I remember a particular evening when a father was desperately trying to get his son to come in and check out our group. I had met this kid already in the main services of our church and while he was a bit awkward, he was easy to talk with and, honestly, delightful. On Wednesday, though, he was showing an obvious fear of being in a room full of teenagers he didn't know. His dad was doing everything to get him to come into our space, but this kid was not having it.

I did my best to help this father out, but to no avail. The kid wouldn't look at me or even acknowledge that I was standing there talking to him. He appeared to be on the verge of a full-on freak-out. I told his dad privately that we might need to try some other things to build up to getting him in to youth group. The situation was just too much of a leap.

I've seen scenarios like this more and more over the years. This is one of many examples of debilitating anxiety in teenagers. Kids today are experiencing strong fears, the types of fears that can be crippling.

And it's not just teenagers. This epidemic spans all ages. Kids are full of fear and adults are full of fear. We live in a fear culture. People and organizations profit from our fear and even try to increase it, whether it's a particular political party getting us to fear the other side or a type of Christian theology getting us to demonize a different position, or even authors who want us to fear what teenagers are going through or getting involved in. Their efforts contribute to us to fearing or even hating the other side, tuning in, and buying more products and books. And some of the most fearful people in the world today are Christians.

I was at In-N-Out a couple of months ago with one of our ninth graders, someone I didn't know very well at the time. He plays baseball on Wednesday nights and rarely makes it to youth group, but we have a fun connection and he comes when he can. So we're sitting there at a table outside enjoying our double-double animal style burgers and I ask him how he's doing.

"Not good," he says.

"What's going on?"

He takes a deep breath. "I'm always afraid."

"Afraid of what?"

THE ANXIOUS TEEN

"Everything. I'm afraid my parents will get divorced. They fight all of the time. I'm afraid that I'm not good enough." His dad had been a professional athlete. "I'm afraid that I'm going to let my dad down. And I'm afraid of what's going on in the world." He paused. "I'm afraid almost all of the time. I feel it as soon as I wake up in the morning."

I listened for a while and took in what he was saying. Then I told him how proud I was of him for telling me and then I began to tell him how fears can lead to other fears but that God wanted to set him free. That he actually was meant to live free of that stuff. I went on to talk about what was behind his fear.

Experts tell us that most fears are based on loss. We fear things because if they happen, we will lose something. So this kid I was talking with was basically saying, *I'm afraid I'll lose my parents. I'm afraid I'll lose their approval. I'm afraid that the things I hear on TV will actually happen. I'm afraid I'll lose my safety.*

So we try to avoid loss. That often causes anxiety. We try to mitigate loss by thinking about how to keep that thing we fear from happening. Often this means we obsess and worry over it from every.single.angle. And that, my friend, is exhausting. For adults. For teenagers. For everyone.

When teens are afraid, they might not act or think rationally. Adults are the same way. For teenagers, this might mean they apply to a million colleges, way more than they need to, because they fear what will happen to their reputation if they don't get into one. They need to get into that certain school and be seen as a success because they have to be in control. Their parents have similar feelings, so they get caught up in trying to make sure their child's reputation is stellar and that all of their plans work out. They join a bunch of club soccer teams or take weeks of SAT prep classes and try to pad their resumés to get into a school that maybe none of them even like.

Control. Mitigate loss. Let nothing unexpected happen.

With the advent of social media and the ever-increasing weight we put on other people's opinions, pressure and fear have intensified dramatically, especially for teenagers. What other people think of their posts, their pictures, and their well-curated life matters beyond what is healthy. In fact, it is everything!

Throw in the fact that the world they are growing up in feels like it's on the verge of falling completely apart. Their parents listen to divisive, one-sided news ad nauseam. At every turn they pick up on an undercurrent of anger and toxicity. The fear tactics are working. And all of it is putting our kids on edge.

As I write this, I'm reading about another school shooting. Another kid taking a gun to school and shooting other students at random.

When we go home and turn on the news, we'll hear about it some more, and a lot of other awful things. In fact, for hours and hours, 24/7, we will hear over and over again that we should all be afraid.

When I feel afraid like this, I can't help but to think about what life was like for the earliest Christians. They lived in a violent, dangerous world—they had just as much to fear as we do, if not more. Yet when we read the old stories out of the Bible, these early believers seem fearless. They are consumed with Jesus's reputation more than their own, more focused on living out God's plan than knowing or controlling every detail themselves. These people lived satisfying and fulfilling lives in spite of danger. Fear did not control them.

These early Christians were persecuted because they were seen as a threat to the Empire. They wouldn't sacrifice to the Roman gods and they were going around saying that Jesus—not Caesar—was Lord. They collected new converts daily because of how dang kind they were, caring for people who were sick and poor, feeding the hungry, taking in orphans, and letting pretty much anyone in on what they were doing.

This quickly-growing group of Jesus followers would not be controlled by the fear of persecution and death the religious leaders and crooked Roman rulers threatened them with. The government grew to view them as a full-on rebellious group, a group pitted against the culture and against Caesar. So the Empire of Rome wanted to squash the early Jesus movement.

But here's the strange thing: The more the government persecuted them, the stronger in their faith these radical Jesus followers grew. Their faith and their movement of love only became more powerful.[54]

A historian described the early Christians this way:

> Christians obey the established law; indeed in their private lives they transcend laws. They love everyone, and by everyone they are persecuted. They are unknown, yet they are condemned; they are put to death, yet they are brought to life. They are poor, yet they make many rich; they need everything, yet they abound in everything. They are dishonored, yet they are glorified in their dishonor; they are slandered, yet they are vindicated. They are cursed, yet they bless; they are insulted, yet they offer respect. When they do good, they are punished as evildoers; when they are punished, they rejoice as though brought to life. By the Jews they are assaulted as foreigners, and by the Greeks they are persecuted, yet those who hate them are unable to give a reason for their hostility.[55]

What would it look like for our students to join this kind of movement? To follow Christ together, to move through the world with spiritual tools to combat fear?

Can you imagine teenagers walking in God's peace and trusting him along the way? Not like some flake with no direction, but like David in the Psalms. Maybe at times screaming, "God, where the heck are you!" (Psalm 77). But then reminding themselves and each other that God is good and he will work out all things for those who love him (Romans 8:28). Remembering that whatever is happening in the world, no matter how things are going, God will guide and lead them (John 16:13).

Imagine if even in the middle of a massive disappointment or a major bout of anxiety they knew deeply who they are and who God really is. How different all of our lives would be if we could always remember that we are children of God and that Jesus, Immanuel, is always with us. That in the end he will make things right.

That doesn't mean we'll never face doubt or that our faith will never waver. Once it has been experienced, anxiety becomes the default for our physiological and psychological self. But if we become captivated by the story of who we are in the context of who God is, we'll begin to have tools with which to combat our default reaction to our fears. When we choose to follow Jesus the old self does not disappear completely, but instead the new self begins to rise up and flourish through the presence of God's Spirit in our lives. And then, with our community, we can face our fears and the questions that spring up because of them.

UNDERSTANDING SUFFERING IN YOUR CIRCUMSTANCE

One night after youth group a group of us were sitting on the floor when a teenager posed this question: "How do I know all of this stuff is true? And if it is true, why won't God fix all that is wrong in the world?"

I love it when students start to ask the big questions. I love it because pat answers do not suffice for this complicated world. Angsty beautiful questions are my favorite! When they come up it means students are beginning to think for themselves, and that's when they become dangerous. Dangerous to small thinking, dangerous to oversimplified answers, dangerous to the enemy who wants to keep them small.

The question made me think again of the first followers of Jesus.

See, the first followers of Jesus had a big advantage. They saw Jesus raised from the dead—something they knew dead people don't do, but somehow he did. About five hundred to a thousand of them got to actually hang out with the risen Jesus for over a month after the resurrection.

He starts teaching them and they begin to grow strong and fearless.

Then Jesus tells them that he is just the first of many who will live eternally. That death will no longer have the final word. And then he calls them into suffering for the cause. To join him in living a life of light in this very dark world. He promises that if they follow him, they'll suffer. He tells them that he will place his Spirit inside of them to give them what they'll need to move forward through this life.

This impacts them deeply in the months and years ahead.

Where anyone else would feel hatred because they were being abused, Jesus would fill his followers with a supernatural ability to love.

Where anyone else would feel deep sadness in the face of huge difficulties, Jesus would come and gently fill his followers with joy.

When his followers were depleted and full of anxiety, Jesus would fill them with his Spirit and give them the kind of peace that passes all understanding.

When others began to oppose them and ridicule them for their beliefs, Jesus would give them the gift of tolerance.

His Spirit would give his followers the ability to be gentle and full of self-control. All of these things would be the evidence that they were truly his followers, that they belonged to a different kind of kingdom. He called these attributes he'd give them the fruit of the Spirit (Galatians 5:22-23).

After he promises all of this to them, he says, "Join me! It's going to be really hard at times, but I will be with you and in you."

And so these people joined him, and they were never the same.

So I'm sitting on the floor with these amazing kids who desperately want to be a part of a movement, but are unsure about what is real. Why? Because the world is broken. More accurately, their world is broken. They are struggling to have faith because God hasn't fixed everything. The world isn't safe. Why is there pain? Why is there suffering? And why do I have to endure it all? Why does anybody?

This is what I wrote about in my book *Youth Ministry 2027*. Helping our kids understand and wrestle with these big questions is so important. If they don't have a robust understanding of suffering, then they will never have a chance to join the movement Jesus is calling us into.

I love how Jesus taught the concept of "already/not yet" to his followers. He would say that the kingdom of God was here and present with them, but then he would also tell them to pray that the kingdom of God would come. There was this idea of the kingdom being already present, but at the same time not quite in its fullness.

Jesus would sometimes heal people and then other times he wouldn't. There would be amazing glimpses of the future kingdom in those miraculous moments—but because of the continued loss and pain of so many others, it was clear how vital it was that the kingdom would come in its fullness one day. Some would be healed, some wouldn't be healed. Some would die and be raised, others would just die. Jesus's followers understood this. And yet, regardless of their circumstances, they could walk in love and freedom.

SHIFTING FROM CIRCUMSTANCE-BASED TO JESUS-BASED

The early church's reliance on God's Spirit neutralized their fear. They knew God's Spirit was present in their lives. They were prayerful and meditative. They prayed without ceasing and did life in community. And God's Spirit gave them peace that passes all understanding.

On top of this—and this point is very important—these early followers' worldview had radically shifted when they met the risen Jesus and when his Spirit filled them. Their priorities went from being based in circumstance and self-preservation to being obsessively focused on Jesus.

Jesus would be their center, regardless of what was happening around them or in their lives, good or bad. They lived in a broken and violent world. But they also knew that Jesus would be with them in the midst of it. This wasn't easy—but this focus shift is what made the early Christians powerful. Unstoppable.

Here's my point: When our up-and-down circumstances determine our beliefs, then we have an erratic, up-and-down belief system. It's just so darn unstable. But if we can help teenagers move away from a circumstantial belief to a Jesus-centered, no-matter-what belief, it will transform their faith and how they are able to deal with fear and anxiety.

A few years ago a student who'd grown up in our church gave her life to Jesus at a winter camp. She seemed to have experienced something radical and amazing. She felt close to her newfound friends in her cabin and was amazed by God's palpable presence. She even got in front of the whole group and shared her story. What she shared was powerful. But literally three weeks later, she was out. Three weeks!! What she'd experienced at camp just couldn't sustain her. The problem was that Jesus hadn't become her center. The difficult circumstance that she returned to when she got home was still her center.

We see similar stories transpire in the Scriptures. The Israelites would see the hand of God, then quickly forget and go on to worship other gods. God fed them each morning with heavenly bread, shaded them with a massive cloud during the afternoon, and provided them with fire to keep them warm at night—yet those incredible and spooky miracles weren't enough to sustain their faith. At least, not right away.

THE POWER OF THE SPIRIT

The early followers of Jesus decided that Jesus would be their center. Together, helping each other, they would reject their need to control and embrace whatever Jesus led them into.

There is a lot in our lives that we can't control. Teens feel this deeply. They have no say in who their parents are, where they grow up, how their family functions, and on and on. Teens feel that lack of self-governance and struggle to gain their voice. The early Christians knew that we are not in as much control of circumstances as we would like to be, but as followers of Jesus we always have access to love, joy, peace, patience, kindness, goodness, tolerance, gentleness, and self-control. Each of us can take heart in this: Regardless of my circumstances and my inability to control everything around me, I know that Jesus lives and the Spirit of God is in me.

I often give students the opportunity to ask the Spirit for what they need. I list out the fruit of the Spirit and give examples for them to think about. It is one of the most beneficial and transformative prayers I get to witness. These students know they are not in control and cannot do life alone. They know they need peace to permeate their fevered, fear-filled minds and take control of their anger. They long to live a life full of the goodness of God with supernatural love oozing out of every pore.

When Jesus is our center, we have access to tools that combat these fears.

Fear of death and separation plagued me as a young person—the idea of losing anyone made me clutch at controlling them and the situation. But as I've grown and gotten to know Jesus, I've come to believe the crazy but true notion that he will never leave us or forsake us (Hebrews 13:5). Everywhere we go he is with us (Joshua 1:9). And all of the anxieties and fears we've acquired over the years can be cast onto this ever-present God because he cares for us (1 Peter 5:7).

The future good news can be lived in this present moment. And when we realize this, in the midst of all the difficulty, God will give us a peace that passes all understanding (Philippians 4:6-7).

CHAPTER TAKEAWAYS

- Many teenagers today experience debilitating levels of fear.
- It's important to allow and make space for our kids to identify and wrestle with their fears and doubts, rather than ignore them.

NOTES *from a Mental Health Therapist*

So how do we help teens not be afraid? How do we help teens believe that Jesus, whom they can't physically touch, is their center? How do we help them hold onto Jesus?

The simple answer, from a therapist's perspective, is to stop trying to convince them to not be afraid, but rather allow space for them to work it out. Saying to

THE ANXIOUS TEEN

a teen "you have nothing to be afraid of" is never helpful.

Trying to talk a teen into trusting Jesus will never be the answer. Trying to convince them that there is no reason to be afraid will fall on deaf ears. But listening to a teen, even in the moments when you don't like what they are saying, will allow them to challenge their own thoughts.

If we sat down with Brock and asked him what made him (finally) believe his parents wouldn't leave and never come back I bet his answer wouldn't be "because they told me so." What changed him was that he saw that they kept coming back. This pattern of his parents returning, coupled with what Brock was learning about Jesus, were both needed for Brock to trust.

Parents who lean into Jesus with fears and doubts have already modeled how to do this to their teens. They've been showing their kids that Jesus is their center. Kids are watching how their parents do life with Jesus.

Listening to your teen, leaving space for them to process their own questions, and modeling a life with Jesus as the center is the best way to help teens find their own path with Jesus.

Programming for Generations Z and Alpha

Around 2010 is when youth workers began noticing more and more kids struggling with social anxiety. There had always been students who felt like youth group wasn't for them, but now we were seeing a whole new level of anxiety and discomfort keeping them from our doors. You could see it on them from a mile away. Their parents would do everything they could do to get them involved in youth group, but it was a no-win situation.

I remember a mom once standing in the back of the youth room with her very obviously upset son at our youth group's Christmas service. It was so clear he did not want to be there, but she had made a deal with him: If he tried it one more time and didn't like it, she'd leave him alone about it. She meant well, but this was not great motivation. He wasn't about to join in and give it a real shot. The mom's face showed that she knew she was in a losing battle. I wanted to rescue her, rescue them, but I couldn't. He just didn't want anything to do with youth group.

I believe there will always be a decent majority of students who thrive in a traditional youth group environment, but there is a growing percentage of kids who are withdrawn and visibly uncomfortable in social settings. I've seen kids who were once super involved and thriving in our group suddenly disappear. They no longer feel safe to come back. It's like they've instantly gone from hot to cold. What is going on?

I'd reach out to those disappearing kids and they'd share that they didn't like their small group or they felt uncomfortable in our larger group settings. When I dug a little deeper, some specifics would come up. Something small might have happened, like a leader asking them to stop hitting people in the face with Nerf balls, or they felt contradicted in small group. In youth groups of the '90s this wouldn't have kept anyone away, but for kids now it can be enough to set them off balance and send them out the door, permanently.

Almost across the board, kids are feeling vulnerable, unsafe, and fragile. As the research we've already looked at shows, because of all the screens, the pressure at school, the busyness, and the noise of their lives, they don't have a regular outlet to decompress. For too many of today's kids, church and youth group just do not feel like a safe place. In fact, for many, it feels like the least safe place in the world.

So how do you program for students who, to varying degrees, are almost all dealing with anxiety and depression?

(RE)INTRODUCE PRAYER AND MEDITATION

When I started rethinking programming in the face of our kids' growing anxiety, the first thing that dawned on me was that we were spending more time doing announcements than we were engaging in prayer. Our students needed to experience the power and presence of God's Spirit. We started to think about how to make that happen.

We began by training our volunteer leaders in prayer exercises like listening prayer. It was vital that our leaders experience God for themselves and grow their own prayer muscles. For many of us Christians, these muscles sit atrophied because of underuse.

In one of these trainings I had us sit in silence for a good five minutes. You ever sat in a room full of people for five minutes without speaking? It can be difficult, to say the least! Before the silence I had us pray an ancient prayer that followers of Christ have been praying for a couple thousand years: "Come, Holy Spirit." And then we waited.

For most of our leaders, the discomfort was extremely high. They had never done anything like spending so much time in a listening prayer exercise, and it felt foreign to them. But a few experienced God's touch. That was enough to motivate us to keep going. One leader told me, "Keep pushing us. We need this desperately. We just don't know it yet." We kept trying. After a few months of this, more of our leaders had sensed God's presence in new and fresh ways. We had begun to learn how to hear his voice more clearly. Our adult leaders were all in! Now it was time to move on to the student leaders.

(By the way—if you're not doing student leadership, I think you're missing the boat big-time. Student leadership is an amazing opportunity to go deeper spiritually in an environment where students are there because they want to be, and because they are longing for more.)

With our student leaders, we did similar things to what we'd tried with our adult volunteers. We also taught them how to pray for each other.

At youth group, we started having these student leaders and adult volunteers stand up front after the talk during the last song. We opened up time for students to come up front and get prayed for by their peers and a leader. Even at this point some of our adult leaders were unsure. They thought it might feel too awkward or embarrassing for kids to come up. I was surprised by all of the negativity from the volunteer team. But I thought, well, we might as well try—what's the worst thing that could happen? And, it worked! So we just kept on doing it. Over time, it got to the point where if we didn't offer prayer after the message, students complained. They felt like they were getting ripped off! Prayer became a centerpiece for us. In a loud and anxiety-producing world, prayer centers us and allows God to break in through all of the noise.

BECOME SMALL GROUP-FOCUSED

The next thing we did was shift to a small group-focused model. So many kids struggle with big group gatherings. We committed to have the majority of our night take place in small groups. (If you are leading a smaller youth group, you have a big advantage in this regard.)

At the beginning of each gathering, we'd immediately place teens in their small groups. We'd begin sitting on the floor in groups eating dinner and then head into the big room with our small groups for a game, worship, talk, and prayer ministry. Then we'd head back into our small groups to end the night. This shift meant we needed to increase the amount of time youth group lasted. Parents initially didn't like the change. Heck, initially *I* didn't like the change—but in the end it really helped us. Focusing on small groups required a bit more time, but it gave more care and attention to individual kids. It helped us to connect more thoroughly and made our time together much more relational. Every night students were in small groups where they were known, cared for, and challenged. We kept hearing from students that their small group was becoming a priority for them. Over time we even noticed that the commitment level to youth group rose because of the importance of small groups. Individual kids felt that they each had a vital role to play in their small group.

IMPLEMENT THE BUDDY SYSTEM

Then, we began a buddy system where we paired adult volunteers with specific students. We knew we had students who were struggling more than the average teenager and needed more intentional contact and care. We wanted to be a place for every type of kid, regardless of their level of struggle. We started training adults to lean into their role as mentor. We have always encouraged leaders to invest once a month into the lives of students outside of regular meetings: seeing a recital or play, watching a kid's soccer game, meeting for coffee, etc. With the buddy system we pushed this even further, assigning leaders to specific students who we knew were struggling, especially with social anxiety. Each of these leaders would spend time with the teenager outside of youth group. Then at youth group when that specific student entered our youth space, their leader was waiting for them. Between our small groups and the buddy system our hope was that no student would ever feel alone. Once we started doing this, the comfort level of our students grew enormously. Kids knew that they would be seen and cared for at youth group. Our group was becoming a safe place for students who rarely felt safe.

CREATE A VIEWING ROOM

Now, there are kids who need a more peaceful, less chaotic space than we can typically provide in our youth rooms. Maybe our music is too loud or the games are too rough or the commotion makes them anxious. With these students in mind, we created a viewing room.

Our church was fortunate to be able to try this thanks to the help of some super techy parishioners. This viewing room became a place where kids could take part in the evening in a smaller, less chaotic space. Students who were really struggling could spend time at youth group in a way that felt safe to them. The room was set up with trained leaders ready to warmly receive students and was stocked with food, crafts, and doodle pads. Most importantly, it was calm and quiet.

From the viewing room students could watch the action taking place in the big group over the screen. Over time this room became a beautiful place where kids felt like they belonged. It grew into its own little community. Sometimes kids who were having a difficult week would go to that space to decompress just for one night, and they'd go back to the big room the next week. Other students went to the viewing room weekly and it became their place. Each student from the viewing room was still in a small group they would join at the end of each program.

All of this went a long way in meeting students where they were. I have to tell you, initially I wasn't for having this separate space at all. It reminded me of the safe space cultures we're seeing on high school and college campuses. At times they might seem overdone or even keep kids from growing into more resilient people. And I also like us all being together. But when I kept hearing from parents that their kid just couldn't make it in our youth room, that convinced me. I'll do whatever it takes to reach and care for any type of kid.

COUNSELING

It's my opinion that today's youth ministry teams must include counselors. Larger churches might have professional counselors on staff, but smaller churches will need to build their own networks of counselors. I have found that most churches have a few counselors and therapists in attendance, so go make friends with them. Share the vision and partner with them to see what kinds of services are available for your students. Counseling can be expensive and, God help us, many families think negatively about counseling. We can help normalize counseling by making it standard in our ministries. We are ministering to a whole generation of kids who are struggling with mental health, and we'll all benefit from bringing in expert help. Ask those experts to help train your volunteer team on how to identify the signs of struggle and how to ask better questions. Consider if you can offer kids counseling sessions at youth retreats or camps. The more students and families experience this, the more it will become the norm and the more students and families will experience the benefits. I also made a point from time to time to mention getting counseling myself. This also de-stigmatizes and normalizes mental health care.

While we are on the subject, make sure to keep a watchful eye on your own mental and emotional well-being. Being in the trenches is taxing. Consistently take time to talk to a mental health professional, seek out healing prayer, meet with a spiritual director, take prayer walks, etc. It's imperative to practice what we preach. The enemy wants to take you down. Don't give up even an inch of your interior life. As one example, my wife and I decided many years ago to go to a marriage counselor once a year whether we felt like we needed it or not. You could do something similar in your marriage or on your own. We all need a tune-up now and again.

DEEPEN YOUR TEACHING

We all know that the stats on kids keeping their faith into adulthood aren't good, and the biblical ignorance is through the roof among believers today. We need to teach students how to think, how to process what they experience in life, and how to make Christ their center. Almost all of us will agree that shallow Christianity isn't cutting it. Deeper teaching doesn't necessarily mean line-by-line and word-by-word teaching of the Bible. Deeper teaching means teaching that leads teenagers toward a deeper understanding of who God is—and then ultimately to God himself.

I love what Paul says about his own preaching in 1 Corinthians 2:4-5: "My message and my preaching were not with wise and persuasive words, but with a demonstration of the Spirit's power, so that your faith might not rest on human wisdom, but on God's power."

When I reflect on Paul in this passage it makes me think that he must have done a lot of work connecting to God's Spirit in preparation for teaching. Kind of crazy that his goal here isn't to get people to be impressed with him and his powerful intellect or his poetry of words. This passage seems to indicate that Paul's preaching didn't lead people to himself and or to Paul's power, but it led the listener to God and his power.

If we solely teach the Scripture and then send teens off to small groups without giving room for them to connect with the God who changes hearts and minds, heals the broken, and gives peace that surpasses understanding, then we are missing the mark.

In our youth group, we found that we were pretty good at talking about God with kids but we weren't very good at ushering them into the *presence* of God. We needed to engage our teens with God's Spirit, and we needed to take care not to lean on the Bible as if it were a member of the Trinity. I know that might not sit well for some of you reading this so I'll say more: The Bible is vital in getting kids to God. It's vital to their learning about him, and it's vital for our teaching. But the Bible isn't God. We must give space for kids to experience his life-changing presence. That might mean providing time for everyone to sit in the quiet or offering individual prayer after the message or responding with a song of worship. We need to avoid relying on our own personalities and our own ability to entertain as the crux of our communication. Instead, we need to prioritize helping our students connect with God.

In the past, our team used to evaluate our speaking like this: "Was it funny?" "Was it engaging?" "Was it intellectually challenging?" These are fine questions, but ultimately what kids are dying for is a connection with the living God.

So we came up with what I think are better questions: "Did students" (those struggling with anxiety, depression, isolation, addiction, and insecurity, as well as those who weren't) "have an opportunity to experience the power and presence of God's Spirit?" "Did what was shared and taught enable them to better understand Jesus and his 'with-ness'?" Beneath these questions was another question: Did what we'd provided that evening challenge their thinking and cause them to grow in respect of the Scriptures AND cause them to have a better understanding of God himself?

If young people only connect intellectually with our teaching, then we're only halfway there. The better way is to let the teaching lead them to sitting in the presence of Jesus, discovering the God who is with them.

In our youth group we talk regularly about what it means to wait on the Lord. In a culture of instant gratification and insta-stardom, our teens do not have a clue what waiting means, especially spiritual waiting. So show them. Create space during your night for waiting, for silence, for listening for the voice of God. Start small—thirty seconds of listening for God's voice seems like an eternity to most. But if you practice making space to wait on a regular basis you'll be able to increase this over time. Teach why waiting is good for our soul and our character. Develop your group's theology of waiting on God.

I like to imagine what would happen if we got better at pairing intellectual teaching with an invitation for God's Spirit to come and work. One of the first times I saw this done really well was at Holy Trinity Brompton Church in London. A theologian from Oxford blew us all away intellectually with his preaching, but he didn't leave it there. After he finished preaching he said, "Now let's invite the Holy Spirit to work in our lives." There was zero manipulation. We just stood up and waited for God's Spirit to work in our hearts and minds. It was the first time I'd experienced something like this in a church. I left that service inspired to continue giving our students deeper teaching, which meant also creating space for deeper connection with God's Spirit.

I want to make space for students to connect with God's Spirit every time I meet with them, even if we just go out for coffee. When we get together like this, yes we have a blast, yes we tell stories, and yes I hope to expand their thinking—but ultimately my prayer is that our conversation and even the silent pauses lead them to Jesus himself. Not the idea of Jesus or teachings about Jesus, but actually to Jesus.

This all can be quite overwhelming. But what if you committed to begin where you are, with one thing? One way of helping students connect with God's presence. Don't worry about changing or adding many things at once. God is with you already. He will bring the people and the resources to care well for the kids in your specific ministry. Start small. Maybe the first step is to just to pray to be open to discovering new ways of meeting today's kids where they are, or to commit to building in a minute or two of silent reflection time during your next gathering. Or maybe have them write a prayer on a piece of paper after your message. Just pick one thing to try and see how it goes. It might be awkward the first time or two, but that's okay. Change isn't easy, but that doesn't mean it's not worth it. Kids are longing for more. So let's give it to them.

CHAPTER TAKEAWAYS

- We need to think beyond traditional program models as we do ministry with kids who are struggling with anxiety and depression.

- We can do this through providing space for meditation, making small groups an important part of every gathering, implementing a buddy system where specific students are paired with adult volunteers or staff, creating a viewing room, partnering our ministries with professional counselors, and deepening our teaching by making space for students to not only hear about God, but experience God's presence.

NOTES *from a Mental Health Therapist*

Can you imagine the impact if every youth worker and volunteer met every teenager exactly where they are? If we could meet a student in their fluctuating needs and provide something that's just right for them, rather than the cookie-cutter version of the Wednesday night youth group that we adults experienced when we were teenagers? Students would feel seen and known and loved.

THE ANXIOUS TEEN

I love the idea of a viewing room. I have worked with countless teens who have gone to youth group out of obligation, often after having a really hard day between school, social dynamics, after school activities, and even family pressure. There are times when any one of us would rather sit at home and rest than go out and be social. The gift of a viewing room on those nights provides respite for teenagers who need it, either every once in a while or every single week. Just as not all students thrive in a traditional classroom, neither will all youth thrive in a traditional youth group. Traditional models do not work for every person every time.

Another way we can meet students where they are is through counseling. There is less stigma around counseling today than there once was, yet many people still often see it as a last resort. Bringing therapists into your ministry on a weekly or occasional basis can make a huge impact in reducing this stigma and providing support for the families who need it.

A related thought: Just as Brock had a great turnout when he offered a class on anxiety, some people will be much more likely to attend a class taught by a therapist than seek individual therapy. In your ministry, try to partner with a therapist who will teach classes for parents. Bring in a therapist to facilitate groups for your students where there can be discussion and resources given around social anxiety or bullying. These relationships will provide someone to go to when you need to talk to a professional about a concern with a student.

Listening Is Love

I was with Tommy, an incredible eighth grade kid. We were sitting at a table, laughing and telling each other our best jokes. He has a great mind and makes everyone laugh, but below the surface I could tell stuff was going on. Whenever I'd turn the corner in our conversation and try to talk about what was happening in his life, he would physically close up. Like, literally, he'd shrink, almost like he was trying to hide. Still, I could sense that he wanted to let me in on what he was going through.

Tommy has a disconnected and angry father. As a punishment for getting a C in English, he woke Tommy up at 3 a.m. and made him run ten miles. He was in fifth grade at the time. Since I met Tommy things haven't been nearly as severe, but they aren't resolved, either. I can sense that something is weighing down this delightful and sensitive kid. Tommy is so conflicted. He desperately wants to be his funny and lighthearted self, but he also seriously wants to please his father—which, by all accounts, will never happen.

I started meeting with him after he began leaving hints, bread crumb trails for me to follow, like coming up at the end of a service and asking me to pray for him, not getting into specifics. Instead he'd say something like, "I just can't do it!"

"Do what?"

"I don't know, just please pray for me."

THE ANXIOUS TEEN

"Okay, dude, let's pray and then let's meet up."

What I've discovered is that when kids realize that an adult takes them seriously and really listens to them, they feel loved. The flood gates open and they feel safe and respected enough to share. It's taken a while, but it's starting to happen with Tommy. For our teenagers, listening is love.

I remember when we crossed that bridge from Tommy hiding to opening the door to what was really going on inside. He and I had hung out a number of times and mostly we just had fun with a little bit of conversation around faith. I had observed enough of his relationship with his father to know that much of his struggles stemmed from that relationship. So finally, one afternoon in Starbucks, I just asked him,

"Tommy, we care for you big-time man, so tell me about your relationship with your dad." And then I just waited.

What happened surprised me.

It opened a flood gate. It was like he just needed permission to share with someone he trusted. We built the trust and I gave him that permission.

My longtime friend Jen is a counselor who has spent her adult life working with teenagers. When I asked her what youth workers need to know about working with kids today her answer was clear: "Tell them to REALLY listen."

When caring adults pursue kids with warm, intentional, and genuinely curious questions, students feel the freedom to share about their lives and what is really going on below the surface. When they feel heard and respected and enjoyed, they will open up about their preferences, desires, and greatest fears, and also their greatest insights and strengths.

In our youth ministries it's imperative that we foster an environment of respect and focused attention. Kids need to know that we truly see them, value them, and want to learn from them. Our whole ministry team of adults has to be on mission in this regard.

When Kelsey became the children's pastor at our church, she left a twenty-five-year career in youth ministry to do so. Initially we both had mixed feelings about it. But I've got to tell you, she's a natural with those younger kids! As they leave the kids ministry service she stands at the door and says to each one of them, "We so enjoyed you this morning! We had a blast with you today!" She is making those kids know that their leaders see and love them, which helps them feel safer to share more about themselves when they come back. As one fifth grader told me recently, "We love Kelsey! She actually listens to us." And what Kelsey does is so simple: She asks them questions and then she listens and enjoys them. Each one of them can tell that she really likes them. What a great kids worker!

Over my thirty-plus years in youth work I have consistently heard from adults who want to join our youth ministry team as volunteers. And their main motivation is that they feel they have a lot to wisdom to give.

Have you heard this? *"Yeah, I just feel like I have so much to teach young people."*

Really? Maybe you do, maybe you don't, but it's a big fat red flag to me. Most of the time the people who say this have never spent any time in actual youth work.

Teenagers do not initially care about what you have to say. You haven't automatically earned the right to drop your truth bombs on them. Typically, leaders who get into ministry because they have wisdom to impart either burn out quickly, or discover that they need to change their approach, beginning a gradual process of listening and learning, then slowly and humbly responding.

In college I remember needing to talk to a pastor, but the pastor I shared with didn't pay much attention. Ever had that happen? We didn't really have a relationship, but I was attending his church and I felt an overwhelming need to share with him how I was struggling with lust. I walked up to him after a Sunday service and began to tell him about this struggle, thinking maybe I could get some advice and prayer. It wasn't an easy thing for me to share. Right off the bat I could tell he wasn't listening very well. He was looking over my shoulder, obviously noticing other people. His attention was divided. I could tell he wanted to get rid of me. I barely felt seen, and the next thing I knew he moved the conversation on to the solution: "Well, just stop. Stop doing that. Stop looking at that stuff." There was no empathy, no connection, no questions. I remember being caught off guard by the abrupt advice and by the abrupt ending to our conversation. I walked away more hopeless than I was before I spoke with the man.

Now I will admit, listening was never my strong suit. Ask my wife. ("Brock, did you hear me? Brock?" Ha!) But I have learned over the years—though I've learned it more slowly than I like to admit—that listening well is one of the most loving things I can do.

I learned as a boy that there's a difference between listening and hearing. Adults told me that hearing is passive and listening is active. I can feel the difference. To listen is to lean in and absorb what is being said. The person speaking can feel and see you listening because of your body language alone.

We learned earlier how babies' brains are shaped by their environment due to a behavior called mirroring. Scientists studying the relationship between listening and good communication have found that when communication is good, the brain waves of the listener and the communicator often begin to sync. Can you imagine that? No wonder kids share the most with the adults who listen to them the most.[56]

Imagine yourself with a student you know is struggling. They feel safe sitting there with you in that coffee shop and then begin to share some troubling things. Maybe about their father. Imagine yourself responding with something like, "Well, at least you *have* a father." Typing that makes me laugh—you wouldn't say that, right? Showing someone the bright side is not the best way to show empathy.

Brené Brown says empathy does not put a silver lining on someone else's experience. Empathy says, *I hear you, and I understand, and I want to sit with you in this thing.*[57] This is the dream, the hope. We hope that every kid we come in contact with feels like we are someone who gets them, listens to them, understands them, and is with them for the journey ahead.

Shortly after confessing to that terrible pastor, I decided I would talk to my mentor instead. I was super nervous to tell him about my struggle with lust. He seemed so holy, and I didn't want him to know that I was an imperfect person. Silly I know, of course he knew I wasn't perfect—just look at me, it's super obvious!—but I was hesitant to be vulnerable, especially after what had happened the last time. Still, I went to my mentor's office and asked to meet with him. Like normal, he dropped everything he was doing and invited me in. I didn't waste time, I just got right into it.

I told him everything and he quietly listened, taking it all in. I could tell he was with me as I dropped all of the ugly on him. When I finished sharing he got on to his knees and with tears in his eyes he said, "Brock, I'm with you and I desperately need Jesus too. Let's pray for each other." I think it might be the only time I cried and hugged a man with both of us on our knees. This was a transformative moment. My mentor listened to my story and empathized with me. This was the first step in leading me to freedom. Long ago I learned about the components of listening through an acronym of the word Listen: **Love, Inquire, Stop, Test, Engage, Nudge.** Let's look at those words and learn how we can listen through the lens of Jesus and how he interacted with people.

L - LOVE

Jesus's motivation was love, and love is the foundation for listening. Jesus said, "Love one another as I have loved you" (John 13:34). When we sit with students, we do it because of love. Any time we're with people, the love of Jesus is what we want to tap into. Even when I stand in front of a church to preach, under my breath I whisper, "Man, I love these people." Love should be our motivation.

I - INQUIRE

Be curious and ask questions. Jesus posed many questions to help the people he was interacting with. He wanted to help them gain clarity and insight for themselves. Ask questions and listen with focused attention. Ask more questions. Listen again.

S - STOP

Take time to stop and make sure you're listening. Jesus was super busy, but always had time for people. Again and again he stopped what he was doing to connect with individual people. People always came before his to-do list.

T - TEST

Sometimes a teenager will say something that isn't exactly what they mean. They're still figuring it out and processing. A good active listener is able to be patient and listen for the core of their message. "The purposes of a person's heart are deep waters, but the one who has insight draws them out" (Proverbs 20:5). Repeat what you think they're saying for clarity, then help them continue to learn how to put words to what they're thinking and feeling.

E - ENGAGE

This can be difficult, but again we can learn from Jesus. Jesus was always in the moment. He was always present with the person he was with. After all, his name is Immanuel—"God with us." He wasn't distracted by the things he had to do later. He didn't interrupt the person who was sharing. People mattered to him, so he listened to them, remaining engaged and present the whole time.

N – NUDGE

You know those moments when you sense that the Holy Spirit's kind of nudging you? The Spirit is leading and directing you. When you're spending time with a student who is sharing with you, you're actually listening intently to two people the whole time: that young person sharing, and God's Spirit. This is when it gets really fun to help people. Heaven and earth were always together in Jesus. You are also a place where heaven and earth meet. You are the dwelling place of God, the temple of the Holy Spirit. This means that when kids are with you, they get a taste of heaven just from being in your presence. They get the incarnation of Jesus sitting there with you. That is powerful.

When you take a teenager seriously and truly listen to them, you give them the gift of honor and respect—a gift that's hard to come by for a teenager today.

CHAPTER TAKEAWAYS

- It's imperative that we foster an environment of respect and focused attention on teenagers. They need to know that we as youth workers and adult volunteers see them, value them, and want to learn from them.

- When students feel heard and respected and enjoyed, they will open up about their preferences, desires, and greatest fears, and also their greatest insights and strengths.

- Kids share the most with the adults who listen to them the most.

- Good listeners are empathetic. As Brené Brown says, empathy does put a silver lining on the other person's experience. Empathetic listeners convey *I hear you, and I understand, and I want to sit with you in this thing.*

NOTES *from a Mental Health Therapist*

Really listening to teens is fascinating, don't you think?

To sit and listen while they navigate life can be so eye-opening. The thing that I want to emphasize, which Brock also alluded to, is how important it is to leave your agenda at the door when you have these conversations. Remember when Brock said kids don't want anyone to tell them what to believe? Well, they don't want to be told your opinions, either. If you are listening to a teen (or anyone, for that matter) with only one ear because you are trying to formulate your response, then you are not really listening.

I encourage you to practice active listening. Active listening is the act of listening intently: listening to the words and hearing what is being communicated. We can't listen intently and formulate our response at the same time. If you find that you are thinking about your response and waiting to say it, then you have stopped listening.

I have worked with lots of teens over my career. I have heard so many times from other adults that teens are hard to work with. But in my experience, teens aren't hard to work with. Teens just want to be heard. They don't want to be told what your thoughts are, they don't want to be told how to do it differently, and they really don't want to be told what needs to be done in order for them to succeed. They want to be truly listened to.

When advising parents, I encourage them to listen in a calm manner. We can practice the same thing in our ministries. Kids who need to talk to their parents or other adults about something important don't want to be met with panic or anger. An abrupt or harsh reaction will shut down conversation. Take the time to practice being calm. When talking with a teen, take a moment to breathe before you speak in *response*—not reaction—to what they say.

If and when you are dealing with excuses from a teen, then respond with a calm, impartial demeanor. Responding this way can be challenging, but it allows for a much more level and helpful conversation than if you react loudly or with any agitation. A loud, opinionated, or upset reaction can cause a teen to put up their defenses, and when the defenses go up, their ability to hear stops. The conversation is dead in the water.

The other day I overheard a mother and son arguing. It wasn't going well. She was angry, he was trying to explain, and communication was at a standstill. Even after she asked him to explain she continued talking over him, sometimes mocking his responses. Do your best to avoid this behavior, no matter how frustrated you might be feeling. If you ask someone a question, wait for the answer without formulating a response, interrupting, or interjecting. If you resort to mocking, then the conversation is over. Take a break, and come back to it later if necessary.

Future Hope

I feel overwhelmed at times, but in the midst of all of the brokenness that I see, I long to live with the perspective that the early church had. The early followers of Jesus lived with ultimate hope. They actually believed that the ending would be good—in fact, really good. They had this great hope even in the midst of intense suffering. This is what I want to hold onto.

Yesterday my wife and I met with a girl in our youth group who is in the middle of a very difficult situation. She is being pressed on all sides. The overwhelming issues in her home would sidetrack any of us, plus she's in the middle of serious drama and difficulty at school. She feels hopeless.

She told us she has this overwhelming feeling in the pit of her stomach that nothing will ever change. You've probably heard students talk like this before. You've probably felt like this yourself. When it feels like darkness is all around and fear lives deep within us, it's very difficult to have a hopeful sense of the future.

When I think about hope and fear, I think about the Old Testament story of Joseph. Everything that could go wrong seems to go wrong for him. He's a kid with a bright future, but then his brothers—because of their own jealousy and probably because Joseph is an incredibly annoying seventh grade boy—sell him into slavery. This is as bad a situation as I can think of, and then bad turns even worse when he is thrown into prison for a crime he didn't commit.

THE ANXIOUS TEEN

Maybe you'd think that Joseph would reject God for all of this trouble. This is what I hear from present-day kids who are struggling. *Why would God allow this? After what happened I don't think I can believe in him anymore.* But in the midst of this hopeless situation, Joseph presses on. This is something I'm not sure I could do.

If I were Joseph I think I'd be done. More than likely I would blame God for what my brothers had done to me. I'd be mad at my brothers too, but I think my anger would ultimately be centered on God. I'd sound a lot like our students sound when difficulty comes their way. But Joseph somehow perseveres. The Bible says that in every difficult and seemingly impossible situation Joseph was forced into, the Lord was with him. I imagine he felt God's presence and it gave him incredible hope. I imagine that he believed God would take people's bad intentions and bring good from them. I imagine this is what sustained Joseph through all of those difficult years. And I know this same kind of hope could change our lives today.

I was hanging with a really good friend of mine a few months ago. We were in the back yard around the fire pit and he was sharing about a legalistic upbringing that had caused him to have an unhealthy fear of hell. "I'm still afraid," he said. "I'm not even sure if I will end up going to heaven. If I'm honest, I don't have a lot of hope for what's next." Imagine that. He loves Jesus, but he also is very aware of himself and his own failures. He kind of believes that his sin is greater than God's goodness. He's gripped by fear.

The hope we can have in Christ is powerful enough to shrink down fear. Hope in God is not wishful thinking. Christian hope is this confidence that what God says will happen will actually take place. God says he loves us. That we are his children, made in his image. God says he is with us always. And when we live life with this sense that he's got us we can breathe deep, knowing that wherever we are right now, the end of the story is good. I know this might sound trite, but there's something for us in this way of seeing life. There's something for our students. God will bring good from this. God will one day make all things right.

THOUGHT LIFE

I tend to daydream a lot. At times my thoughts are dark and hopeless, but most often they are warm and hope-filled. Sometimes I think about the future kingdom breaking in and when I do, my fear and anxiety usually calm down. This imagining of the future is an amazing exercise that consistently fills me with peace and hope and even joy. I believe that God is good. I truly believe that when I stand before him, even his correction will feel like love.

Not all of our students know the love of God yet. They don't all trust in what he has for them. As youth workers, we get to be the ones who keep telling them about this unending, limitless love. We get to tell them about the Christian hope for the future, and how that hope changes how we live in this present moment.

ULTIMATE HOPE

I can see it all happening. Jesus back, making all things right again. There I am, standing there face to face with Jesus. I can see the whole thing in my mind's eye. He and I will be standing on the beach together, away from the hustle and bustle of the celebration. I'll tell him about when I fell in love with Kelsey and how when we had our amazing daughter Dancin, I cried my eyes out with joy.

I'll ask him if he remembers when I became plagued with anxiety and really struggled. With warmth he'll say, "Oh yes, Brock, I was there."

He'll tell me how proud of me he is and how he loved that I persevered through it all. Through the abuse by his good people. Through the bad decisions that led to worse decisions, and how I stayed at it in this not-so-easy calling.

I'll ask him if he remembers how my parents talked about me to him all of the time. How they woke up every day and prayed for me. How they carried the burden with me. I'll ask if he saw how I was never alone. How I did it all in partnership with Kelsey and Dancin and how that was my favorite part. He'll smile and say, "Yeah, mine too. I loved watching the three of you together."

With a grin on my face I'll ask, "Do you remember when that middle school boy threw poop at that other middle school boy on that retreat in Palm Springs?" We'll laugh hard together over that one. "Yeah, and remember after that when that kid got hit directly in the eye with a full fire extinguisher? Oh, he was so paranoid that his retina had gotten detached!" he'll say. "Oh, I laughed at that one." I'll shrug my shoulders. "Oops," I'll add with a smirk.

He'll talk about some of his favorite parts of my life. We'll stand there looking at the water together, remembering. He'll say, "Remember when I sent that manatee to save you from drowning?" (That's a story for another day.) We'll both laugh together while looking out at the sea. He'll turn and put his hands on both of my shoulders and with a warm smile he'll say, "You did so good Brock. You were so faithful. Well done."

I think I'll cry in that moment. I'll look at him and just thank him. I'll thank him for loving me so much. For being patient with me. For calling me and using me. For staying with me the whole time. I'll say, "I'm just so very grateful that I don't think I have the words to express it." He'll look at me and say, "Brock, you don't need any. I totally get it and I love it."

We'll walk back to the party together and join the great reunion of all of us and of heaven and earth. I can hardly wait.

CHAPTER TAKEAWAY

- We can trust that Jesus is with us through everything we have experienced and will experience. Jesus is there loving us, caring for us, rooting for us, and bringing out the best in us. His love is greater than any fear or anxiety, and we will never be without it.

NOTES *from a Mental Health Therapist*

Amen.

Epilogue: You are the Right You

There has never been a more critical time for ministering to teenagers. Youth ministry is desperate for savvy, wise, seasoned ministers.

The last five to ten years have been my most effective as a youth pastor. Why? Because I finally kind of know what I'm doing. Kids are leaning in and listening to me because they know that I love them and will listen to them about everything—their worries, their mistakes, their low points, and their joys. Their parents pursue me and listen to me because I've put in the time. I've dedicated my life to young people, to their parents, and to other youth workers and I've loved it all.

That's not to say that there aren't a lot of challenges and obstacles for longtime youth workers like me. Maybe you've felt what I've felt at times: discouraged, overwhelmed, stressed out, and hopeless—wondering if it's all worth it. And so I thought I'd give you an important reminder at the end of this book on kids and anxiety:

You have a vision for who kids are and who they are becoming, and you make church the safest place on Earth for students. Safe to screw up, safe to make mistakes, safe to doubt the faith, safe to confront their sexuality, safe to be at their worst, safe to be anxious and depressed. And why? Because that's what Jesus did for you and me! He extended his extravagant grace to us. We know he listens to us and welcomes us just as we are. We are compelled to extend the same grace and love to all of the hurting young people around us.

THE ANXIOUS TEEN

Teenagers right now are filled with so much anxiety and fear that they can barely face the thought of tomorrow. This generation doesn't feel safe anywhere. They don't feel safe at home, they don't feel safe online, and they even struggle feeling safe with their friends. But somehow with you, they're safe.

Not long ago we were in Jamaica on a mission trip with Praying Pelican Missions. Out of nowhere one of the students sitting next to me inhaled deeply and quietly said, "I haven't felt this safe in my entire life."
Youth ministry creates environments where students can experience the warmth and peace of God. We actually extend this to them through our very presence. God's warmth travels with us everywhere we go. In the midst of their struggles, anxieties, and self-doubt, teenagers are drawn to those who show them that we not only love them, but actually like them, echoing God's heart for them.

God has given us as youth workers insight into this messy and complex culture and he has filled us with his Spirit, which enables us to see truth wherever it is.

I am convinced that a movement is just around the corner. It's dark right now, but dawn is about to break. And this movement is going to begin with our youth. It's why there's no way on earth I'm getting out of youth work. I want to stay on the front lines and I hope that you stay in it with me.

Know this: You are not alone. There's a community of radicals all over the world giving our lives to this next generation. We're a family, a tribe of people who don't quite fit in other places.

We are colleagues and collaborators joining up with Jesus's kingdom work in youth culture, one of the darkest places on earth. We belong to this calling and we belong to each other.

So breathe deep.

If you're ever in a room of youth workers just know you're safe.

- Safe to laugh.
- Safe to vent.
- Safe to be yourself.
- Safe to say what's really on your mind.

We get it. You don't need to explain yourself.

Youth workers are the people who are connecting with this hurting generation, in coffee houses and football fields, at parks and at burger joints, in churches and in schools. We are the ones who know what's really going on in the lives of young people today. And that's why we've got to stick with these kids and this youth ministry calling, even through the deep challenges. The world has never been more desperate for thoughtful, caring, and well-trained adults who will journey with young people who are struggling profoundly.

And you are one of the ones God has called! Somehow God saw you and thought, "Holy me! You'd be an amazing youth worker."

You get to be part of this divine thing. You get to carry this gospel to an incredibly broken world of kids—kids who are worried, confused, struggling, and lonely. You were called for such a time as this. You get to move with them through anxiety toward hope, love, and meaning. This is the right time and you are the right you.

THE ANXIOUS TEEN

Appendix: Prayer, Breathing, Meditation, and Other Exercises

I was speaking in Buffalo, New York, at a parent conference a few years back. I love to encourage, inspire, and challenge moms and dads in their mission as parents. After one of the sessions on teen anxiety and depression, a priest from a local parish came up and said, "You know, if you added Buddhist meditation into your presentation, it would be even more powerful and wholistic." I was caught off guard, but I thanked him and went on with the day. I couldn't shake what he said, though. Not because I didn't like it, but because the truth in it challenged me. I think also it bugged me that he would think we'd need to go to Buddhism to find good meditation. The next day I started reading the Scriptures, and what he had said kept spinning in my mind. I started looking for the prayers and mentions of being still and waiting on the Lord, seeking out references and examples of meditation. It was all there in the Bible—but I hadn't really focused on these practices before. The truth in what that priest shared with me became powerful. I needed to help kids learn how to breathe and pray and sit and wait.

Years ago I attended a contemplative youth ministry talk at the National Youth Workers Convention led by one of my favorites, Mark Yaconelli. In the seminar Mark led us through some spiritual disciplines so that we youth workers could take time to connect to Jesus ourselves and then be equipped to lead our students into a greater sense of the Holy Spirit's presence. This was one of the greatest seminar experiences I've ever had. I left understanding how a meditative life could benefit my own relationship with Jesus and how I could lead students into the deeper waters of faith. This is the secret to ministry: We pursue Jesus ourselves and call others to join us in the pursuit of him.

Practicing the presence of God each day, meditating, and doing prayer and breathing exercises have been a huge part of my healing in my own anxiety journey. My hope for students, particularly those who are experiencing anxiety, is that they would know God's presence in similar ways.

Christian meditation isn't just a thing that we should think about doing, it's a command for us. Joshua 1:8 says, "Keep this Book of the Law always on your lips; meditate on it day and night, so that you may be careful to do everything written in it. Then you will be prosperous and successful."

Or how about Psalm 4:4: "Tremble and do not sin; when you are on your beds, search your hearts and be silent."

As youth workers it's vital that we learn to live life connected to God, even in the midst of our busy and stressful days. From there, we simply invite students into this way of living with us.

What follows are a number of practices that we can use ourselves and with our students. My prayer is that these practices will lead us into a deeper connection with God's Spirit and therefore the fruit of the Spirit begins to bubble up in our lives.

MEDITATION ON SCRIPTURE

God has given us the Scriptures to reveal himself to us so that we might know him better and love him more. As we seek to enjoy fellowship with God by pondering the words of Scripture, the Holy Spirit opens our hearts to experience greater depths of his love. The Spirit also strengthens us by helping us more fully grasp "how wide and long and high and deep" Christ's love is, deepening our roots in his love (Ephesians 3:18-19). Meditating on Scripture is one way that we "keep seeking the things above, where Christ is" (Colossians 3:1). It is a conscious engagement of the mind with God. This renewing of the mind (Romans 12:1-2) is part of the process by which the word of God penetrates the soul and spirit with the light of illumination and the power of transformation.

Meditation also removes us from the center—the location where we like to see ourselves—and places Christ firmly in the place of provider. Remember all that "Jesus as center" stuff I talked about before? Focused times of contemplation are one way we keep an awareness of what it means to have spiritual connectedness to God. As Philippians 4:6-7 says, "Do not be anxious about anything, but in every situation, by prayer and petition, with thanksgiving, present your requests to God. And the peace of God, which transcends all understanding, will guard your hearts and your minds in Christ Jesus."

When we meditate on Scripture, there can be this deep connection between what our minds take in and what our hearts receive. God is longing to reveal himself to us, and meditation can be used to bring us into a more relational connection to God through his Word. It engages both the mind and the heart.

RECOMMENDED SCRIPTURE VERSES

The following Scriptures are meaningful when read aloud slowly, individually or as a group. Typically I might read them two or three times, emphasizing certain words as I feel led, helping those struggling to relax and begin engaging with the text.

Philippians 4:6-7
Do not be anxious about anything, but in every situation, by prayer and petition, with thanksgiving, present your requests to God. And the peace of God, which transcends all understanding, will guard your hearts and your minds in Christ Jesus.

1 Peter 5:7
Cast all your anxiety on him because he cares for you.

Isaiah 41:10
So do not fear, for I am with you;
   do not be dismayed, for I am your God.
I will strengthen you and help you;
   I will uphold you with my righteous right hand.

John 14:27
Peace I leave with you; my peace I give you. I do not give to you as the world gives. Do not let your hearts be troubled and do not be afraid.

Proverbs 3:5-6
Trust in the Lord with all your heart
and lean not on your own understanding;
in all your ways submit to him,
and he will make your paths straight.

Psalm 55:22
Cast your cares on the Lord
   and he will sustain you;
he will never let
   the righteous be shaken.

Colossians 3:15
Let the peace of Christ rule in your hearts, since as members of one body you were called to peace. And be thankful.

Philippians 4:19
And my God will meet all your needs according to the riches of his glory in Christ Jesus.

DEVELOPING A PRAYING CULTURE

When we seek God in the midst of our anxious thoughts, we are essentially surrendering our place as ruler of our own life and handing it back over to him. We admit our need, our inability to control situations and people, and our perspective shifts. In return, he offers us supernatural peace and preservation of our inner life. Exactly what we need!

PRAYER, BREATHING, AND OTHER EXERCISES

The following are a number of prayer and breathing exercises that you can use with your group. I encourage you to practice these exercises yourself first. I also warn you to not let any discomfort you feel keep you from engaging your students with these. There will always be a few who resist these types of practices. In my experience some adult leaders struggle more than kids. That is okay. Be kind, but move forward. Make this space for teenagers to experience God's presence, without apology. We are in the business of spiritual formation, so let's get on with it! For every one person who is uncomfortable with it or who is "not feeling it," there will be two or three who sense God in a completely new way.

Kelsey uses these prayer and meditation exercises with elementary kids in her role as family ministries director. She has cool stories every week about how God speaks to these children and reveals himself to them, even at their young age. She has created a safe space for children to experience the presence of God through the gift of their imaginations. Start them young and keep it up. Normalize making space to hear from God and speak to him.

CENTERING ON CHRIST

This is one of the prayers I learned from Mark Yaconelli. When I lead it for youth, I usually demonstrate first. Then I say something like this:

"We are going to pray a focused prayer together. I'll say a line and then you repeat the line out loud together. This prayer exercise involves movement, so move your hands where I move mine."

(both hands in middle of chest)
    Christ be in my life and in my living (audience repeats)
(both hands over heart)
    Christ be in my heart and in my loving (audience repeats)
(both hands over mouth)
    Christ be in my mouth and in my speaking (audience repeats)
(both hands over eyes)
    Christ be in my eyes and in my seeing (audience repeats)
(both hands over ears)
    Christ be in my ears and in my hearing (audience repeats)
(both hands on top of head)
    Christ be in my mind and in my thinking (audience repeats)

"Now we're going to do the same thing except this time I will say the prayer alone—don't repeat after me. Just quietly move your hands along as I pray through it a couple of times. Pause at those areas of your life where you sense you need to give something over to the Lord. Maybe you've been struggling with your words. Pause at that point and give that area of your life over to the Lord."

Pray through the prayer again.

"…When you're ready to move on just look up at me." (Continue once the room is ready.)

Imagine being in a room full of students who are learning how to slow down and use words to ask Jesus to come into every aspect of their lives. It's a powerful scene! Kids have told me that they also pray this prayer at night or in the midst of difficulty. A college freshman home on break told me that she made some terrible decisions her first semester. One night she remembered this prayer. She got down on her knees in her dorm room and prayed it from memory, and she immediately sensed that Jesus was present with her. This is what spiritual disciplines do for us.

Kids don't want us to tell them what to believe. That approach shuts down the mind. These disciplines reengage their minds by giving them tools to help them pursue spiritual discovery on their own. Our goal is to move kids beyond rational thought to a place where they can experience the person who sets them free.

HOLY SPIRIT PRAYER
Here's another quick prayer we do with our students:

> "I place my hands open on my lap and pray, 'Come, Holy Spirit.'" (pause)
> "I place my hands on my ears and pray, 'Give me ears to hear you.'" (pause)
> "I place my hands upon my eyes and pray, 'Give me eyes to see you.'" (pause)
> "I place my hands on my heart and pray again, 'Come, Holy Spirit.'" (pause)

THE IMMANUEL PRAYER
Our ministry has used several variations of this prayer. We have prayed it in a large group and we've prayed through it with individual students. This prayer focuses on the truth that we can rely on God's nature as Immanuel, which in Hebrew means "God with us" (Isaiah 7:14). By his very character, he is always everywhere, personally present. That means God was with us before we were Christians and even during our worst moments. It means

that God is with us now, whatever our circumstances, and will always be with us.

The intent in the Immanuel Prayer is to help people connect personally—not just theoretically—with the God who is present. This prayer is interactive and can be prayed in both positive and difficult experiences.

On the left of the diagram below, students think back to a time they enjoyed or felt loved, a positive experience. They invite Jesus into that specific moment in their memory, engaging with him to see what else he might want to reveal to them. Often this leads the participant into a sense of safety, making a deeper place of hurt or trauma more accessible. This takes them to the right side of the diagram where they repeat the process. Again, they invite Jesus into that circumstance or situation and explore where Jesus was in it. It changes their perspective and shifts their center from the circumstance to the realization that Jesus was with them the whole time.

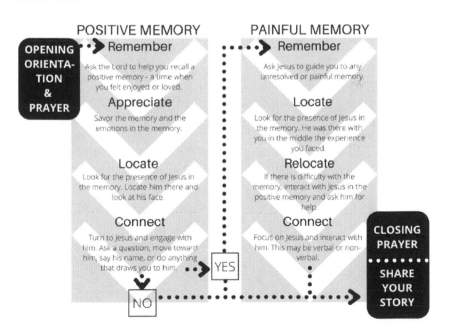

The Immanuel Prayer. Image created by Kelsey Morgan.

THE ANXIOUS TEEN

JESUS ON THE THRONE

This prayer exercise Mark Yaconelli taught in his seminar is all about visualizing Jesus on the throne. We've done this one with our kids and they absolutely love it. I'll do my best to explain how it works:

Dim the lights and have students kneel and close their eyes.
Tell them to picture themselves bowing before Jesus, who is sitting on the throne.

Ask:

"What does he look like?
How is he looking at you?

Now, see him reaching down to touch the top of your head to bless you.
Bow your head before him.

Now, raise your head and look up at him in worship.

I'll know you're ready to move on when you open your eyes and look at me."

Debrief with your students. Let them know that it is okay to not see/feel anything. Affirm whatever you get—trust the Spirit to keep working.

PRAYER FOR SOOTHING PANIC ATTACKS

The following prayer is intended for panic attacks. You can adapt it to pray over a student or to pray for a group of students, or an individual can pray this on their own while experiencing intense anxiety. This would be a great resource to give students who are struggling with panic attacks so they can refer to it as needed.

"Dear God,
I come before You to lay my panic and anxiety at Your feet. When I'm crushed by my fears and worries, remind me of Your power and Your grace. Fill me with your peace as I trust in You and You alone. I know

I can't beat this on my own, but I also know that I have You, Lord, and You have already paid the ultimate price to carry my burdens. For this I thank you, Amen."[58]

Prayer from Psalm 27

Leading students in times of group prayers can be powerful and stabilizing. I use this prayer in a corporate time of prayer, pausing and having students use their own words after each section.

"Dear Jesus,

"You are the strength of my life; you are my rock, my fortress and my protector; therefore, of whom shall I be afraid?" (Pause and instruct students to take a few seconds to pray into that theme using their own words.)

"You are my shield, my strong-tower and my stronghold. I will call to you because you are worthy to be praised." (Pause and instruct students to take a few seconds to pray into that theme using their own words.)

"So, Father, I thank you for being my strength and my God in whom I trust." (Pause and instruct students to take a few seconds to pray into that theme using their own words.)

"Amen."

—Adapted from Psalm 27:1b[59]

Prayer for Confronting Fear

This is a great corporate prayer to use with teenagers to invite God into the worry of their lives.

"Heavenly Father,
When I feel crushed by my own worries,
Lift my mind and help me to see the truth.
When fear grips me tight and I feel I cannot move,
Free my heart and help me to take things one step at a time.

When I can't express the turmoil inside,
Calm me with your quiet words of love.
I choose to trust in you, each day, each hour, each moment of my life.
I know deep down that I am forgiven in your grace, restored by your
sacrifice. You have set me free.
Amen."[60]

PRAYER FOR CALMING A TROUBLED HEART

I was teaching on the theme of God being with us when we are troubled
in our hearts and minds. After the teaching I led our students through this
corporate prayer:

"Loving God,

Please grant me peace of mind and calm my troubled heart. My soul
is like a turbulent sea. I can't seem to find my balance so I stumble and
worry constantly.

Give me the strength and clarity of mind to find my purpose and walk
the path you've laid out for me. I trust your love, God, and know that
you will heal this stress. Just as the sun rises each day against the dark of
night.

Please bring me clarity with the light of God.

In your name I pray, Amen."[61]

PROGRESSIVE MUSCLE RELAXATION

Progressive muscle relaxation, which occurs during breathing exercises, can
help release muscle tension and put a pause on worrying. The technique
involves systematically tensing and then releasing different muscle groups
in your body. As your body relaxes, your mind will follow. When I have
done this it really has helped me.

EXPRESSIVE ACTIVITY

The mind and body have a really cool relationship, and they work best
when they support each other. Often, though, our mind and body are

not working together positively. Sometimes they even work against each other. Our body could be walking in a beautiful forest while our mind is obsessing about the thing we wish we'd said in that awkward conversation earlier today. But what's cool is that when the mind and body are on the same page, we are present. One of the main goals of these breathing and prayer activities is to help students become more present with and aware of their mind, body, and spirit. When the whole person is present with a pleasant experience, the nervous system automatically begins to let go of stress and tension—which is always a good thing.

We'll all benefit from looking for ways to process what we and our students are learning or what we're stressing over through activities that are good for our nervous system. These activities help to bring the mind and body in sync, which leads to more calm and peace. Possibilities include coloring, going for a walk, shooting hoops, or listening to music.

AN APP TO DOWNLOAD: LECTIO365
Another great resource is Lectio365, which prompts users to have regular, daily times of prayer. Encourage your students to download the Lectio365 app. These regular prompts from their smartphones can be really helpful reminders. The app is amazing—plus the readers all have British accents, so yay!

BREATHING EXERCISE
Described by Hallie

The symptoms of panic attacks often feel like the symptoms of hyperventilation. People experiencing a panic attack often feel dizziness, shortness of breath, and numbness, along with other symptoms.

For a person experiencing these symptoms, it can be hard to know what to do. Panic attacks can feel frightening. In a panic attack, it can be helpful to sit down. Sit against something solid, such as a wall or a sofa, or even on the ground. Feel the solidness around you and breathe.

Breathe in for five counts.
Hold for three counts.
Breathe out for five counts.

Repeat for as long as you'd like.

THE 54321 GROUNDING METHOD
Described by Hallie

The 54321 grounding method is another strategy to use when faced with feelings of intense anxiety.

Find and name five things you can see. For instance: trees, cars, clouds, a chair, a picture, your shoe.

Then, name four things you can feel. Maybe the wind. The sun. The air conditioning in the room. The fabric of your clothing.

Then name three things you can hear. Are people talking? Are birds chirping?

Then name two things that you can smell. A candle? Food on the stove? The scent of a rainstorm?

Lastly, name one thing you can taste. If you can't come up with anything for this, you can name one taste you really like.

PRACTICES FOR WHEN YOU'RE EXPERIENCING PANIC
Described by Hallie

When experiencing panic, it's helpful to keep your thinking in the present. Many times our anxiety comes out of trying to figure out the future—trying to solve problems that haven't occurred yet. Stay focused on the moment you're currently in. As the Bible says, "Therefore do not worry about tomorrow, for tomorrow will worry about itself. Each day has enough trouble of its own" (Matthew 6:34).

Sometimes if you're feeling anxious the best step is to shut down your thinking. Stop the loop that is running through your brain. How do you do this? Try changing what you're focused on. You can do this by talking with God, listening to music, playing a game, or turning on a movie. Any of these steps can help to change the story that's running through your mind and allow you to reset.

Mindfulness and meditation work well for some people in managing anxiety. Keep in mind that sometimes being mindful and aware doesn't supply enough deflection to get the mind out of its loop. That doesn't mean you aren't doing meditation correctly; it just means that right now your brain needs something different. Try one of the other strategies, and come back to mindfulness and meditation another time.

Acknowledgements

First I want to thank Hallie for her thoughtful contribution to this book. We met a couple of years ago at a dinner party and hit it off right from the get-go. I actually asked her on the spot if she'd join me in this huge undertaking. I'm so grateful to her for saying yes and for her partnership in this. But Hallie, I'm still waiting for an invite to Hawaii. Come on!

A big thank you to my amazing wife, Kelsey, and our spectacular daughter, Dancin. I love you both so stinking much. Thank you for journeying with me through my own bouts of anxiety. Thank you for your patience and your love during those times. I'm thunderstruck with gratitude! And thank you for your partnership in investing in this next generation. I am flat-out the most blessed husband and father on the planet because of the two of you.

A big fat thank you to my parents. They heard I was writing this book and started reading all kinds of books on the subject. Their help in shooting me ideas and quotes and research—well, let me just say, I have an amazing mom and dad. I love you both so much and I'm grateful for your help and encouragement. Now let's go to Disneyland!

Marko, I'm super grateful for your friendship and for how you have believed in me all of these years. I love you, bro!

I've worked with Sarah Hauge before this project, and as an editor, there just isn't much better. Sarah, I'm so thankful for your patience, your kindness but also for pushing me past where I wanted to be pushed. It was painful at times but I'm so grateful for you!

In the first chapter I spoke about a student counselor who met with me and honestly saved my life. His name is Jim Gaffney. Jim, thank you big-time, my friend. Let's grab coffee soon!

Jenifer Morrison has been a great friend of mine for over fifteen years now. Jen, I love you, I'm proud of you, and I thank you for your contribution to my life and to this book. And thank you for regularly taking care of C.S. Lewis for us. He loves you the most!

I'm grateful to Chris Butler, Ph.D. for coming to our youth group and not only teaching our students how to find relief from anxiety, but also helping me in a big way. Chris, thank you for your generosity and for your insightful ministry.

A shout out to Mike Erre and his work on Alexander the Great. He inspired me to dig in deep there. Much appreciation, Mike!

I am grateful to be at a church that allows me to write and speak and use my gifts. If you're ever in the Southern California area on a Sunday, you should stop in. The Holy Spirit is doing an amazing thing there. I love you, Bridge family—let's keep representing and extending the reign of Jesus everywhere we go!

Lastly and specifically I must say that I love the youth leaders at The Bridge and the students in our youth group so much. I'm just so thankful to be able to do life with each of you. I love you all big-time and I'm so fortunate to have each one of you are in my life!

ENDNOTES

1. Chap Clark, *Hurt 2.0: Inside the World of Today's Teenagers* (Grand Rapids, MI: Baker Academic, 2011).

2. Jeff Orlowski (dir.), *The Social Dilemma*. Exposure Labs, 2020. https://www.netflix.com/title/81254224?source=35.

3. Ariane Resnick, "Can You Be Addicted to Dopamine?" *Verywell Mind*. November 30, 2021. https://www.verywellmind.com/can-you-get-addicted-to-dopamine-5207433.

4. *The Social Dilemma.*

5. "How Does Social Media Affect Teenagers?" *Newport Academy*. July 14, 2021. https://www.newportacademy.com/resources/well-being/effect-of-social-media-on-teenagers/.

6. N. Darvesh, A. Radhakrishnan, C.C. Lachance, *et al.*, "Exploring the prevalence of gaming disorder and Internet gaming disorder: a rapid scoping review." *Syst Rev* 9, 68 (2020). https://doi.org/10.1186/s13643-020-01329-2.

7. "Teenagers and Sleep: How Much Sleep Is Enough?" *Johns Hopkins Medicine*. https://www.hopkinsmedicine.org/health/wellness-and-prevention/teenagers-and-sleep-how-much-sleep-is-enough.

8. "Constantly Connected: Adverse Effects of Media on Children & Teens." *Healthy Children*, from the American Academy of Pediatrics. Last updated October 7, 2016. https://www.healthychildren.org/English/family-life/Media/Pages/Adverse-Effects-of-Television-Commercials.aspx.

9. David Kinnaman and Mark Matlock, *Faith for Exiles: 5 Ways for a New Generation to Follow Jesus in Digital Babylon* (Grand Rapids, MI: Baker Books, 2019).

10. Clark, *Hurt 2.0*

11. Bronwyn Williams, "Prescribed Play for Generation Alpha." *Flux Trends*. https://www.fluxtrends.com/prescribed-play-for-generation-alpha/.

12. Robert Murray et al., "The crucial role of recess in school." *Pediatrics* vol. 131,1, 183-8. 2013. doi:10.1542/peds.2012-2993.

13. Daniel J. Siegel, MD, *Brainstorm: The Power and Purpose of the Teenager Brain* (New York: Jeremy P. Tarcher/Penguin, 2015).

14. Joshua J. Mark, "Protegoras of Abdera: Of All Things Man Is The Measure." *World History Encyclopedia*. January 18, 2012. https://www.worldhistory.org/article/61/protagoras-of-abdera-of-all-things-man-is-the-meas/.

15. N.S. Gill, "Roman Exposure of Infants." *ThoughtCo.* February 2, 2019. https://www.thoughtco.com/roman-exposure-of-infants-118370.

16. G. van N. Viljoen, "Plato and Aristotle on the Exposure of Infants at Athens." *Acta Classica* 2 (1959): 58–69. http://www.jstor.org/stable/24591098.

17. Vanessa Caceres, "Eating Disorder Statistics." *U.S. News.* February 14, 2020. https://health.usnews.com/conditions/eating-disorder/articles/eating-disorder-statistics.

18. "10 Statistics of Teenage Eating Disorders." *Polaris Teen Center.* June 12, 2018. https://polaristeen.com/articles/10-statistics-of-teenage-eating-disorders/.

19. "The Scary Truth About Teen Eating Disorders: Causes, Effects, and Statistics." *Newport Academy.* July 28, 2017. https://www.newportacademy.com/resources/mental-health/scary-truth-teen-eating-disorders/.

20. PSC Media Wire, "Americans Spent Over $9 Billion on Aesthetic Plastic Surgery in 2020!" *The Plastic Surgery Channel.* April 7, 2021. https://www.theplasticsurgerychannel.com/2021/04/07/americans-spent-over-9-billion-on-aesthetic-plastic-surgery-in-2020/.

21. "Any Anxiety Disorder." *National Institute of Mental Health.* https://www.nimh.nih.gov/health/statistics/any-anxiety-disorder.

22. This chapter was inspired by an anxiety class taught by Chris Butler, Ph.D.

23. "Students Who Feel Emotionally Unprepared for College More Likely to Report Poor Academic Performance and Negative College Experience." *The Harris Poll.* https://theharrispoll.com/the-jed-foundation-partnership-for-drug-free-kids-and-the-jordan-porco-foundation-today-released-the-results-of-a-national-first-year-college-experience-survey-exploring-the-challe/.

24. Claire McCarthy, MD, FAAP, "Anxiety in Teens Is Rising: What's Going On?" *Healthy Children.* November 20, 2019. https://www.healthychildren.org/English/health-issues/conditions/emotional-problems/Pages/Anxiety-Disorders.aspx.

25. Will Meek, Ph.D., "Generalized Anxiety Disorder and Self-Esteem." *Verywell Mind.* September 19, 2019. https://www.verywellmind.com/anxiety-and-self-esteem-1393168.

26. "Did You Know?" *Anxiety & Depression Association of America.* https://adaa.org/understanding-anxiety/facts-statistics.

27. Ibid.

28. Ibid.

29. "Brain Development." *First Things First.* https://www.firstthingsfirst.org/early-childhood-matters/brain-development/.

30. Daniel J. Siegel, *Mindsight: The New Science of Personal Transformation* (New York: Bantam Books Trade Paperbacks, 2010).

31. Siegel, *Mindsight.*

32. Bessel A. van der Kolk, *The Body Keeps the Score: Brain, Mind, and Body in the Healing of Trauma* (New York: Penguin Books, 2014).

33. PTSD often occurs after really difficult experiences, experiences like many of our kids have gone through during the pandemic. Although research continues, EMDR remains controversial among some health care professionals. Personally, I've seen it work.

34. "Teen Suicide." *Stanford Children's Health.* https://www.stanfordchildrens.org/en/topic/default?id=teen-suicide-90-P02584.

35. Jones SE, Ethier KA, Hertz M, et al. Mental Health, Suicidality, and Connectedness Among High School Students During the COVID-19 Pandemic — Adolescent Behaviors and Experiences Survey, United States, January–June 2021. MMWR Suppl 2022;71(Suppl-3):16–21. DOI: http://dx.doi.org/10.15585/mmwr.su7103a3external icon.

36. Dennis Thompson, "Big Rise in Suicide Attempts by U.S. Teen Girls During Pandemic. *U.S. News and World Report.* June 11, 2021. https://www.usnews.com/news/health-news/articles/2021-06-11/big-rise-in-suicide-attempts-by-us-teen-girls-during-pandemic.

37. Ibid.

38. "Even before COVID-19 pandemic, youth suicide already at record high." *UC Davis Health.* April 8, 2021. https://health.ucdavis.edu/news/headlines/even-before-covid-19-pandemic-youth-suicide-already-at-record-high/2021/04.

39. "Understanding the Characteristics of Suicide in Children." *National Institute of Mental Health.* December 14, 2021. https://www.nimh.nih.gov/news/research-highlights/2021/understanding-the-characteristics-of-suicide-in-young-children.

40. "Talking to Teens: Suicide Prevention." *American Psychological Association.* April 19, 2018. https://www.apa.org/topics/suicide/prevention-teens.

41. Kara Gavin, "Fewer Deaths Among Adults Who Got Extra Support as Suicidal Teens." February 14, 2019. *Lab Log* at Michigan Medicine. https://labblog.uofmhealth.org/rounds/fewer-deaths-among-adults-who-got-extra-support-as-suicidal-teens.

42. Lilia Mucka Andrew and Erin M. Sadler, "How to Help a Child with Suicidal Thoughts." *Rise and Shine*. September 10, 2019. https://riseandshine.childrensnational.org/how-to-help-a-child-with-suicidal-thoughts/.

43. Ibid.

44. Juliana Menasce Horowitz and Nikki Graf, "Most U.S. Teens See Anxiety and Depression as a Major Problem Among Their Peers." *Pew Research Center*. February 20, 2019. https://www.pewresearch.org/social-trends/2019/02/20/most-u-s-teens-see-anxiety-and-depression-as-a-major-problem-among-their-peers/.

45. As quoted in Jon Payne, "The Pastor's Prayer Life." *Ligonier*. September 15, 2018. ligonier.org/learn/devotionals/pastors-prayer-life.

46. Sonya Deschênes, Michel Dugas, Katie Fracalanza, & Naomi Koerner. (2012). The Role of Anger in Generalized Anxiety Disorder. Cognitive behaviour therapy. 41. 261-71. 10.1080/16506073.2012.666564.

47. Alice G. Walton, "7 Ways Meditation Can Actually Change the Brain." *Forbes*. February 9, 2015. https://www.forbes.com/sites/alicegwalton/2015/02/09/7-ways-meditation-can-actually-change-the-brain/?sh=c3b72bf14658.

48. Richard Rohr, *Soul Brothers: Men in the Bible Speak to Men Today* (Maryknoll, New York: Orbis Books, 2004).

49. "Personal Narrative" (1739), from The Works of President Edwards (1830) Vol. I, Extractions from his Private Diary, 27-28, Published by Sereno B. Dwight.

50. Paul Woolley, "John Stott listened and made the church relevant in the modern world." *The Times*. https://www.thetimes.co.uk/article/john-stott-listened-and-made-the-church-relevant-in-the-modern-world-h0bmgbdms.

51. "42 Quotes About Meditation," *Christian Quotes*. https://www.christian-quotes.info/quotes-by-topic/quotes-about-meditation/.

52. The Falls Church Anglican, "Being Human." https://www.tfcanglican.org/being-human.

53. "Types of Phobias: Where They Come from and How to Treat Them." *Newport Academy*. January 12, 2018. https://www.newportacademy.com/resources/mental-health/types-of-phobias/.

54. Matthew J Thomas, "Suffering and Persecution in Early Christianity." *Word & World*. May 23, 2017. https://en.ifesjournal.org/suffering-and-persecution-in-early-christianity-518e73b29d8b. Candida Moss, *How an apocalyptic plague helped spread Christianity*. CNN. June 23, 2014. http://religion.blogs.cnn.com/2014/06/23/how-an-apocalyptic-plague-helped-christianity/.

55. As found in *Diognetus;* Diog. 5.10–17, https://en.ifesjournal.org/suffering-and-persecution-in-early-christianity-518e73b29d8b.

56. RR Romeo, JA Leonard, ST Robinson, et al., "Beyond the 30-Million-Word Gap: Children's Conversational Exposure Is Associated With Language-Related Brain Function." *Psychological Science.* 2018;29(5):700-710. doi:10.1177/0956797617742725.

57. RSA, "Brené Brown on Empathy." *YouTube.com.* December 10, 2013. 2:53. https://www.youtube.com/watch?v=1Evwgu369Jw.

58. Olivia Muenter, "18 Calming Prayers for Anxiety That Offer Instant Stress Relief." *Woman's Day.* December 9, 2021. https://www.womansday.com/life/inspirational-stories/g29613781/prayers-for-anxiety/.

59. Ibid.

60. Ibid.

61. Ibid.

Made in the USA
Columbia, SC
09 August 2022

64926586R00107